Electronic Projects fc

GUITAR

Electronic Projects for GUITAR

RA Penfold

PC Publishing

PC Publishing
4 Brook Street
Tonbridge
Kent TN9 2PJ

First published 1992
© PC Publishing

ISBN 1 870775 31 7

British Library Cataloguing in Publication Data
Penfold, R. A.
    Electronic Projects for Guitar
    I. Title
    787.87
    ISBN 1-870775-31-7

Composition by Scribe Design, Gillingham, Kent
Printed and bound in Great Britain by Thomson Litho Ltd, East Kilbride

Contents

Preface

1 Getting started *1*

2 Guitar projects *30*

Guitar preamplifier *30*

Headphone amplifier *34*

Soft distortion effects unit *37*

Compressor *42*

Auto-waa *46*

Waa-waa pedal *50*

Phaser *53*

Dual tracking effects unit *58*

Expander *63*

Treble booster *69*

Dynamic treble booster *73*

Dynamic tremolo *76*

Direct injection box *81*

Improved distortion unit *85*

Thin distortion unit *88*

Guitar tuner *91*

Glossary *97*

Index *109*

Preface

Home made equipment has been part of the electronic music scene for just about as long as there has been electronic music. In the early days there was often no alternative to using home constructed equipment since ready made alternatives were conspicuous by their absence. Also, the commercial electronic music gear that was available tended to be quite expensive. Today's ready-made electronic instruments, guitar effects units, etc. are much more affordable, but in many cases it is still possible to produce home constructed units for significantly less than the cost of broadly comparable ready made alternatives. It is also still possible to build effects units etc. that have no true commercial counterparts.

Whether you wish to save money, boldly go where no guitarist has gone before, rekindle the pioneering spirit, or simply have fun building some electronic music gadgets, the designs featured in this book should suit your needs. The projects are all easy to build, and some are so simple that even complete beginners at electronic project construction can tackle them with ease. (The preamp, headphone amp, soft distortion unit, expander, treble boost and DI box are particularly suitable for beginners.) Stripboard layouts are provided for every project, together with a wiring diagram. The mechanical side of construction has largely been left to individual constructors to sort out, simply because the vast majority of project builders prefer to do their own thing in this respect. All the designs are suitable for any normal guitar pick-ups, both high or low output types. None of the designs requires the use of any test equipment in order to get them set up properly. Where any setting up is required, the procedures are very straightforward, and they are described in detail.

Getting started 1

T he projects featured in this book should present few difficulties to anyone who has some previous experience of electronic project construction. In fact many of the projects are simple enough for complete beginners to electronics, but there is some essential background information that must be acquired before anyone new to this type of thing starts soldering in earnest. In this chapter it is not possible to provide a complete course on electronic components, methods of construction, etc. What is provided is an introduction to the components, construction techniques, etc. that are needed in order to build the particular projects described in this book.

With this information, a certain amount of skill, some common sense, and a bit of ingenuity, practically anyone should be able to build the more simple of the projects. If you are not a very practical sort of person, then I would be misleading you to say that you could still complete these projects successfully. It would not be true either, to say that an average beginner could successfully tackle the more complex of the projects featured in this book. However, provided you are not completely useless when it comes to manual skills, and you start with the simple projects first, it should not be too difficult to build these projects.

Components

The range of electronic components currently available to amateur users is vast. There are literally thousands of different components available. Fortunately, only a fairly small percentage of these are used in the projects featured here (see Photos 1 and 2). This makes it relatively easy to obtain and identify the components. If you do not already have one of the larger electronic component mail order catalogues, then I would strongly advise getting at least one of these before starting to buy any of the components for a project.

If you are lucky enough to live near a branch of one the large electronic component retailers, then you may be able to obtain everything you need locally. Even if this should be the case, it is still worthwhile having one or two large electronic component catalogues. These contain a mass of useful data, and also have lots of photographs or drawings of the components. These are very useful for beginners, as

1

Photo 1
A Resistor
B Radial electrolytic capacitor
C Ceramic capacitor
D Axial electrolytic capacitor
E Polyester capacitor
F Preset resistor

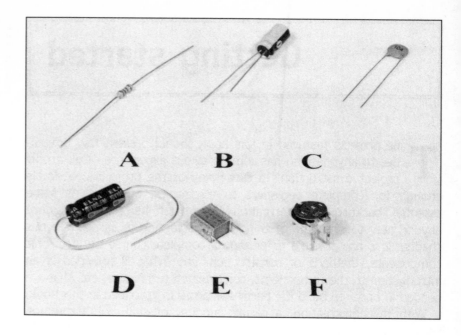

Photo 2
A Diode
B Transistor
C LED
D 8 pin DIL IC
E 14 pin DIL IC
F 16 pin DIL IC

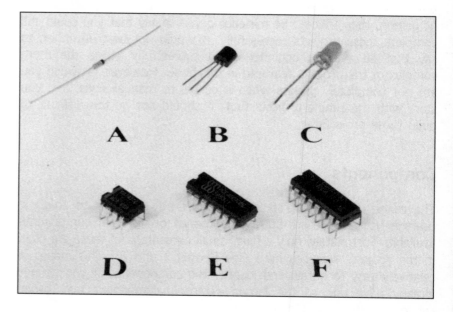

they make it relatively easy to find the right components. To put things another way, it reduces the risk of wasting time and money buying the wrong thing. If you do not live near to a suitable shop, then a big electronic components catalogue and mail order buying represent the only practical method of obtaining the components you will need for these projects.

Resistors

Resistors must be the most common of electronic components. Practically every electronic project uses some of these, and in most cases they represent about half the components in a project. There are numerous different types of resistor available, but for most of the projects in this book ordinary carbon film resistors will suffice. You may find that some suppliers do not sell carbon film resistors. This is normally where they have rationalised their resistor stocks, and offer the higher quality metal film type as their bog standard resistor.

The extra quality of metal film resistors is unlikely to bring any significant benefits with most of the projects featured here, but it will obviously not do any harm either. Metal film resistors are perfectly suitable for these projects, but where carbon film types are available they will do the job just as well but at a much lower cost. For the DI box project I would recommend the use of metal film resistors, but even with this project carbon film types will work quite well.

The values of resistors are specified in ohms. The greek letter omega (Ω) is still used as an abbreviation for ohms, but these days a capital R is more commonly used. Thus a 10 ohm resistor will often be referred to as a 10R component. In fact a value of 10R, particularly on circuit diagrams, is often just given as 10. An ohm is a very small unit, and many of the resistors used in electronics have values of thousands of ohms, or even millions of ohms. One thousand ohms equal one kilohm, and the abbreviation k is often used for kilohms. A million ohms is a megohm, or just M.

A 33000 ohm resistor would therefore normally have its value given as 33 kilohms, or just 33k. A 1500000 ohm resistor has a value of 1.5 megohms, or just 1.5M for short. The letter which indicates the unit in use is often used to indicate the decimal point as well. Thus a 4R7 resistor is a 4.7 ohm type, a 5k6 resistor is a 5.6 kilohm (5600 ohm) component, and a 1M8 resistor is a 1.8 megohm (1800000 ohm) type. The point of this system is that it enables values to be represented using as few digits as possible. This is especially useful when trying to find space for the labels on circuit diagrams.

Resistors are available only in certain values, known as preferred values. This is what is generally known as the E24 series of values:-

1.0	1.1	1.2	1.3	1.5	1.6
1.8	2.0	2.2	2.4	2.7	3.0
3.3	3.6	3.9	4.3	4.7	5.1
5.6	6.2	6.8	7.5	8.2	9.1

This series might look a little odd, but it operates on the principle of having each value about 10% higher than the previous one. This ensures that whatever the calculated value for a resistor might be, there will always be an actual value available that is within a few percent of it. Note that components are not just available in these values, but also in their decades. In other words, as well as (say) 2.2 ohm resistors, there are also 22R, 220R, 2k2, 22k, 220k, and 2M2 types available. Resistors are not generally available with values higher than 10M, and so you will probably not find 22M types listed in components catalogues.

Resistors have a tolerance rating, and this is usually 5% (possibly 10% on the higher values). The actual value of a resistor is never precisely its marked value. The tolerance rating is merely an indication of the maximum error. For example, a 100k 5% resistor would have an actual value of between 95k (100k minus 5%) and 105k (100k plus 5%). Ordinary 5/10% resistors are fine for the projects in this book. If your component supplier sells metal film resistors as their standard type, then these will have a tolerance of just 1% or 2%. These are a bit over-specified for our purposes, but are otherwise perfectly suitable for use in these projects.

Last, and by no means least, resistors have a power rating. This is basically just the maximum power in watts that the resistor can withstand. Practical power ratings tend to be a bit misleading as they are often quoted for different operating conditions. A 0.6 watt resistor might have a power rating that represents something close to the point where the component burns up, whereas a 0.25 watt type might have a rating that represents a very safe maximum dissipation figure. Their real power handling ability might therefore be quite similar, despite the fact that the power ratings are very different. For these projects 0.25 watt resistors will suffice. Higher power types, such as 0.33, 0.4, 0.5, and 0.6 watt types are also suitable, provided they are miniature types. Resistors such as old style 0.5 and 1 watt resistors are fine from the electronic point of view, but you are unlikely to be able to fit them into the component layouts provided here!

Colour coding

It is very unusual for resistors to have their values marked in numbers and letters. The standard method of value marking is to have four coloured bands. This method of coding works in the manner shown in Figure 1.1 and Table 1. In theory, the first band is the one nearest to one end of the resistor's body. I would have to say that with all the small resistors in my spares box the two end bands are an equal distance from their respective ends of the body. However, it is still easy enough to tell which band is which, as the fourth band is well separated from the other three.

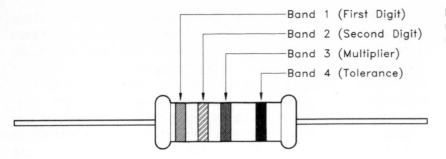

Band 1 (First Digit)
Band 2 (Second Digit)
Band 3 (Multiplier)
Band 4 (Tolerance)

Figure 1.1 The standard four band method of marking values onto resistors

Table 1 Resistor colour coding

Colour	Band 1/2	Band 3	Band 4
Black	0	x1	–
Brown	1	x10	1%
Red	2	x100	2%
Orange	3	x1000	–
Yellow	4	x10000	–
Green	5	x100000	0.5%
Blue	6	x1000000	0.25%
Violet	7	–	0.1%
Grey	8	–	–
White	9	–	–
Gold	–	–	5%
Silver	–	–	10%
None	–	–	20%

The first two bands indicate the first two digits of the value. For example, if these bands are respectively green and blue, the first two digits are 5 and 6, as can be seen from Table 1. The third band is the multiplier, and this basically just indicates the number of zeros that must be added to the first two digits in order to give the full value. For instance, if the third band is orange, this indicates that the first two digits must be multiplied by 1000, or that three zeros must be added in other words. Thus in our example value, we have 56 plus three zeros, or a value of 56000 ohms (56k). Band number four indicates the tolerance of the component. This will usually be gold, which indicates a tolerance of five per cent.

This colour coding system can be a little confusing at first, but it has the advantage that the value markings are not easily obliterated. Even if the coloured bands should become chipped or worn, there will probably still be enough left to permit the value to be reliably deciphered. With tiny lettering on miniature resistors, it would be difficult to read the values even if the lettering was in perfect condition.

There is a slight problem with resistor colour coding in that there are also a couple of five band codes in use. These are closely based on the standard four band type. With one of these five band codes you have what is basically the ordinary four band code, plus an extra band which indicates the temperature coefficient. The latter is a measure of how much the component's resistance changes with variations in temperature. This is something that is not normally of any interest, and the extra band can be ignored. There is an alternative (and rare) five band code which has the first three bands to indicate the first three digits of the value. The last two digits indicate the multiplier value and tolerance in the normal way. If a retailer is selling resistors with one of these five band codes, then their catalogue should give details of the code in use.

Potentiometers

A potentiometer is a form of resistor whose value can be varied. A normal potentiometer has a control shaft which is fitted with a knob (see A and C in Photo 3). There is also a mounting nut and bush so that it can be fixed to the front panel of the case. For the projects featured here it is the small carbon potentiometers (type C) that are required, not high power types such as wirewound potentiometers. Usually the mounting bush is for a 10 millimetre diameter hole, and the control shaft is 6 millimetres in diameter. However, some modern potentiometers have smaller mounting bushes and (or) shafts. Some, for instance, have the standard 6 millimetre shaft diameter, but require a mounting hole of just 7 millimetres in diameter. These miniature types are suitable for the projects featured here provided

Photo 3
A Miniature potentiomete
B Miniature toggle switch
C Potentiometer
D Rotary switch
E Standard jack socket
F Heavy duty push-button switch

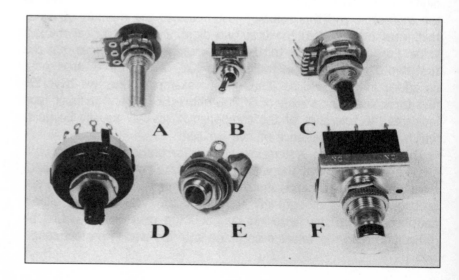

you remember to make the smaller mounting holes that they require. It is probably best to avoid types which have a control shaft diameter of other than 6 millimetres unless you are sure that you can obtain control knobs to fit them.

As far as their electrical characteristics are concerned, there are two types of potentiometer. These are the logarithmic (log) and linear (lin) types. A linear potentiometer is the normal kind, where setting the control at a roughly mid-setting gives about half maximum resistance. A logarithmic potentiometer has a very non-linear resistance characteristic. Adjustment towards one end of the track has little effect, while adjustment at the opposite end results in large changes in value. Logarithmic potentiometers are mainly used as volume controls, while linear potentiometers are used for practically all other potentiometer applications. The components lists always specify which type is needed. Using the wrong type will not prevent a project from working, but you will get some strange control characteristics. This can make the projects difficult to use properly, so I would strongly recommend that the specified types should always be used.

Preset potentiometers are physically very different from the standard variety. These are small components, and are often of open construction. Fortunately, it seems to be increasingly common for these components to have a plastic outer casing to keep dust and other contamination away from their inner workings. For these projects it is the sub-miniature (0.1 or 0.15 watt) horizontal mounting type that is required. Other types are suitable electrically, but will probably not fit into the component layouts properly, and could be very expensive in the case of high quality multi-turn types.

Preset potentiometers are generally available only as linear types incidentally. Because of this, components lists do not normally specify whether a preset should be a logarithmic or a linear type, and component catalogues do not normally specify the type either. Unless stated otherwise, preset potentiometers can be assumed to be linear types.

Note that colour coding is not normally used for marking potentiometer values. Instead, the value is simply marked as 4k7 lin, or whatever. In some cases a letter A after the value is used to denote a logarithmic component, or a letter B is used to shown that it is a linear type. Colour coding is occasionally used for marking values on preset resistors. This coding is normally in the form of three coloured dots which indicate the value in the same way as the first three bands of a normal resistor colour code.

Capacitors

Capacitors represent another type of component that is used in large numbers in electronic circuits. In a few projects they actually outnumber the resistors. The values of capacitors are in farads, but one farad is a massive amount of capacitance. Therefore, most real world capacitors have their values marked in microfarads, nanofarads, or picofarads. Table 2 shows the relationship between these three units of measurement. A microfarad is one millionth of a farad incidentally. The abbreviations u, n, and p are often used for microfarads, nanofarads, and picofarads respectively.

Table 2   Relative values of capacitors

Unit	Microfarads	Nanofarads	Picofarads
Microfarads	1	1000	1000000
Nanofarads	0.001	1	1000
Picofarads	0.000001	0.001	1

There are numerous different types of capacitor available (see Photo 1, page 2). Here we will consider only the types that are relevant to the projects in this book. Where low values are called for, by which I mean values of under one nanofarad, ceramic plate capacitors are suitable. These are very small, square, plate-like components with the two leadout wires coming from one edge of the component. The values are usually marked in picofarads on the very low values (e.g. 27p = 27 picofarads). Values of more than 100 picofarads are sometimes marked in a slightly cryptic fashion, with the value being given in nanofarads. Thus n10 is 0.10 nanofarads or 100 picofarads, and n39 is 0.39 nanofarads or 390 picofarads. This is basically the usual method of using the units indicator to also show the position of the decimal point, but no leading zero is included.

There can be a problem with ceramic plate capacitors in that some of the components currently being sold have very short leadout wires indeed. In some cases these will fit into the component layouts without any difficulty, but in a few cases it might be necessary to solder short extension wires to their leadout wires in order to fit them into the component layouts properly.

Polystyrene components are also suitable where values of under one nanofarad are called for. The only proviso here is that they must be physically small types. There should be no problem if modern components are used, and you do not order a type intended for operation at very high voltages. The values of small polystyrene capacitors are normally marked on the components in picofarads, possibly with the tolerance shown as well, or a code letter to show the tolerance. Ordinary 5% tolerance polystyrene capacitors are suitable for these projects.

For values from one nanofarad to around one microfarad the component layouts are designed to take printed circuit mounting polyester capacitors. These have very short leadout wires that are really more like pins than normal leadout wires. This means that the component layouts have to be designed to suit components of a particular lead spacing. In this case a lead spacing of 7.5 millimetres (0.3 inches) is used for virtually all the medium value capacitors. Check the component layouts and be careful to order components that have the appropriate lead spacing.

It is only fair to warn you that the likely result of trying to manipulate polyester capacitors which have the wrong lead spacing into these component layouts is that leadout wires will become detached from the capacitors. In days gone by these polyester capacitors were very easily damaged in this way. Modern types seem to be much tougher, but they are still likely to be damaged if you bend the wires to suit a different lead spacing.

The values of polyester capacitors are normally marked on the components in nanofarads or picofarads, as appropriate. A 2.2 nanofarad component would therefore be marked 2n2, a 10n component would be marked 10n, and a 470nf (0.47uf) component would be marked u47.

In a few cases ceramic capacitors are specified for values of around 100 nanofarads. These higher value ceramic capacitors have very inaccurate values, but they work well at high frequencies. This makes them well suited to certain applications, including decoupling types. It does not matter which type of ceramic capacitor is used, but disc types are the most widely available, and are generally the cheapest. Obviously you should avoid very high voltage types, or any special ceramic types which are expensive or physically quite large.

The value of ceramic capacitors is often just marked in nano or microfarads. Probably the most common method of value marking though, is one which uses three numbers. The first two numbers are the first two digits of the value. The third number is the number of zeros that must be added to these in order to give the value in picofarads. For a 100 nanofarad capacitor the marking would be 104. The first two digits of the value are 1 and 0, and four zeros must be added to these. This gives a value of 100000 picofarads, which is the same as 100 nanofarads.

Electrolytics

Ordinary capacitors are not a very practical proposition where high values of more than about one microfarad are required. They are expensive to produce, and tend to be physically quite large. For high values it is normal to use electrolytic capacitors. These are not without their drawbacks, such as relatively high tolerances and high leakage currents, but they are adequate for many purposes where high values are needed. The most important difference between electrolytic and non-electrolytic capacitors is that the electrolytic type are polarised. In other words they have positive and negative terminals, and must be connected into circuit the right way round if they are to function properly. Ordinary capacitors such as polyester and ceramic types, and resistors, can be fitted either way round.

Identifying the positive and negative leadout wires should not be difficult, since there are usually + and − signs marked on the body of an electrolytic capacitor which clearly show which lead is which. There seems to be a tendency these days towards marking only one lead or the other, but this is obviously all you need in order to get the component fitted round the right way.

Physically there are two different types of electrolytic capacitor. These are the radial and axial types. These are actually general terms which are applied to other types of component, but which are mainly encountered when dealing with electrolytic capacitors. An axial type is the usual tubular bodied component having a leadout wire protruding from each end. These would normally be mounted horizontally on the circuit board. A radial component has both leadout wires coming from the same end of the component, and it is intended for vertical mounting. It is usually possible to fit a radial capacitor into a layout that is designed for an axial type, or vice versa. Some careful forming of the leadout wires may be needed, or some extension wires might have to be added to the leadout wires.

It is best to avoid this type of thing though. Apart from the fact that it will give some slightly scrappy looking results, it is likely to result in components being something less than firmly fixed in place. This leaves the board vulnerable to problems with broken leads or short circuits from one component lead to another. Incidentally, you will notice that axial electrolytics have an indentation around one end of the component's body. This is used to indicate the end of the component from which the positive (+) lead emanates. The + and (or) − markings are usually included as well, but the indentation enables you to see the polarity at a glance, making these markings largely superfluous.

Incidentally, radial capacitors are also know as PC (printed circuit) capacitors. This is actually a term which can be applied to any component which is intended for vertical mounting on a printed circuit board. In the early days of electronics all two lead components were of the axial type. When printed circuits came along, these vertically mounting components were designed specifically to give compact component layouts with the new method of construction. Hence these became known as printed circuit mounting components, and eventually just PC components.

With non-electrolytic capacitors you do not normally need to worry about the maximum voltages they can safely handle. The voltage ratings are generally around the 100 volt mark, or in some cases even higher. The projects in this book mostly operate on a 9 volt battery supply.

The situation is slightly different with electrolytic capacitors. The smaller values generally have voltage ratings of about 50 volts or more, but the higher values can have voltage ratings as low as 6 volts, or possibly even 3 volts. The components lists therefore give voltage ratings for electrolytics that are the minimum requirements. Any voltage ratings equal to or higher than these are suitable, provided the components are physically small enough to fit into the available space. If a 1u 10V component is specified, there should be no difficulty in using a 1u 100V type, which (if it is a modern component) should be physically quite small. On the other hand, you are unlikely to get away with using a 220u 100V component where a 220u 10V type is specified. A capacitor having such a high value and operating voltage would almost certainly be quite large.

Note that with the lower values of around 1u to 10u, most component suppliers no longer list components having low operating voltages. There is then no option but to opt for components having operating voltages of around 50 to 100 volts. These should be physically small components though, and they should fit into these component layouts with no difficulty.

Diodes

A diode is a type of semiconductor (like transistors and integrated circuits, see photo 2, page 2), but is the most simple type of semiconductor. It acts like a sort of electronic valve which enables an electric current to flow in one direction, but not the other. These components are also called rectifiers. The only difference between a rectifier and a diode is that the former is used in medium and high power applications, whereas a diode is used for small signals. Only diodes are used in the projects featured in this book.

Obviously a diode or rectifier must be connected the right way round if it is to let the current flow in the right direction. The standard method of polarity marking for diodes and the smaller rectifiers is to have a band marked around one end of the component's body. This indicates the cathode (+) leadout wire. The component layout diagrams in this book show this band on all diodes, so all you have to do is fit these components onto the board so that they match up with the diagrams in this respect. You do not really need to worry about what the terminals are called.

Diodes, like all semiconductors, do not have values. Instead they have type numbers, and the data sheet for each component shows its electrical ratings and characteristics. To make it easier to find the particular semiconductor you require, most component catalogues list diodes, rectifiers, transistors, etc. separately. The diodes used in these projects are all very common types which you should be able to find listed in any electronic components catalogue.

It is worth mentioning here that semiconductors are rather more vulnerable to heat damage than are most other electronic components. Modern silicon devices are somewhat more hardy in this respect than the old germanium based devices. However, even the silicon based devices need to be treated with due respect when they are being soldered into circuit. You can buy an implement called a heat-shunt. This clips onto leadout wires, and removes much of the heat that flows up the wires towards the bodies of components when soldered joints are being produced. I have never found it necessary to use one of these, but I do make sure that every soldered joint is completed fairly rapidly. If it becomes evident that a joint is not proceeding well, it is better to abandon it and try again once everything has cooled down, rather than pressing on and possibly damaging the component.

You are unlikely to use any germanium semiconductors apart from diodes. These have electrical characteristics which still make them preferable to silicon diodes in certain applications. When using these components you should obviously be especially careful to avoid overheating them. Again, there should be no need to use a heat-shunt, but complete each joint as swiftly as possible.

It is worth bearing in mind that no electronic components are totally heat-proof. Even with simple components such as resistors you can cause damage if you keep the bit of the soldering iron in place for so long that the component becomes discoloured and smoke begins to rise! Components will often survive this sort of treatment, but often with shifted values or other problems that will degrade performance. Try to complete all soldered joints reasonably quickly, preferably taking no more than a second or two.

Transistors

The components discussed so far have all been two lead types. Transistors have three leadout wires, or in a few cases four leads (see Photo 2, page 2). The circuits featured here use only the normal three leadout variety. The terminals of a transistor are called the base, emitter and collector (often just abbreviated to b, e and c respectively). The component layout diagrams featured in this book do not necessarily include identification letters for the leadout wires of transistors. This is simply because in most cases it is obvious how the component should be fitted onto the board if you look at the diagram and the component itself. Simply fit the components with the orientation shown in the diagrams, avoiding any crossed-over leadout wires. Note that where a leadout diagram for a transistor is shown, it is the convention that a base view is shown (i.e. the component is shown looking onto the leadout wires).

One of the projects in this book uses a special type of transistor called a VMOS type. The leadouts of these, and other field effect transistors (f.e.t.s) are called the drain, gate and source. However, once again there is no need to worry too much about the names of the leadout wires. Just mount the transistor so that its orientation matches the component layout diagram.

In many component catalogues there are dozens or even hundreds of different transistors listed. The transistors used in the projects featured here, apart from the VN10KM VMOS transistor, are all very common types. These should be listed in any electronics component catalogue, and should be amongst the cheapest of the transistors in the catalogue. Transistors are normally listed in the catalogues in some sort of alpha-numeric order, so it should not be too difficult to locate the right type numbers. The VN10KM is available from some of the larger component retailers.

Integrated circuits

Modern electronic circuits tend to be extremely complex – even the simple ones. This might seem to be an impossible state of affairs, but it is made possible by integrated circuits. Strictly speaking each integrated circuit is a single component. However, it actually contains the equivalent of what could be anything from two to over one million components. Although a project might only use a dozen components, two of these could be integrated circuits, each containing the equivalent of hundreds or thousands of components. This brings tremendous benefits to the electronics hobbyist. Many projects that would otherwise be impractical are brought within the scope of many constructors. Integrated circuits can be used to reduce component counts to a realistic level, and also help to keep down costs. Very simple projects that actually do something useful become a practical proposition.

Some integrated circuits are quite cheap, and cost a matter of pence rather than pounds. Where possible, the projects in this book are based on low cost devices that are available from practically every electronic component supplier. In a few cases there is no choice but to opt for specialist devices that are less widely available and more expensive. Where a device is not widely available, the components list will mention one or two sources.

There are many hundreds of integrated circuits listed in most components catalogues. In order to make it easier to find the devices you require it is standard practice for the integrated circuits to be listed in several categories. Most of the devices used in these projects are linear integrated circuits. The only non-linear types used in these projects are 4000 series CMOS logic devices. Any component catalogue should have a CMOS logic section which lists the appropriate devices. As there are many instances of totally different integrated circuits which very similar type numbers, you need to be careful when ordering these components.

Another point to bear in mind is that the same device might be produced by two or more manufacturers, but under slightly different type numbers. There is a popular linear device called the uA741C. I believe that this was the type number used by the original manufacturer, and it is still specified as such in many components lists, including some of those in this book. However, it is now produced by several semiconductor manufacturers, under type numbers such as LM741C, MC741C, and CA741C.

In components catalogues a device such as this might be listed under one specific type number, or even two or three different type numbers if the retailer stocks components from more than one source. In many cases though, popular integrated circuits which are produced by several manufacturers are simply listed under a sort of generic type number, which in this example would just be 741 or 741C. Where necessary, the text for a project will include advice which should help you to find the right component.

Integrated circuits come in a variety of sizes and shapes (see Photo 2, page 2). Many devices are available in more than one encapsulation. However, in component catalogues you will normally only find the d.i.l. (dual in-line) versions listed. These are basically rectangles of black plastic which contain the silicon chip, with a row of metal pins along each long edge of the plastic case. It is from these two lines of pins that the d.i.l. name is derived. Most integrated circuits have 8, 14 or 16 pins, but they can have anything from four to forty or more pins. The projects featured here only have 8, 14 or 16 pins though.

Some integrated circuits are built using some form of MOS (metal oxide silicon) technology, and the practical importance of this is that they are sensitive to static voltages. A large static charge could probably damage any integrated circuit, but charges of this magnitude are not to be found in normal environments. MOS components can be damaged by relatively small static charges, such as those that tend to be generated by nylon carpets, clothes made from synthetic fabrics, etc. The risk of components being damaged in this way has perhaps tended to be exaggerated slightly. Manufacturers warnings can give the impression that MOS devices will be instantly destroyed unless they are stored and handled under carefully controlled conditions using thousands of pounds worth of specialised equipment!

In reality the risk is normally quite small. Many electronics hobbyists do not bother with any special handling precautions at all when dealing with MOS components, and in the main get away with it. However, when dealing with the more expensive MOS components it would seem to be prudent to exercise reasonable care. In fact it is not a bad idea to take a few simple precautions even when dealing with the cheaper components.

The most important of these is to leave static-sensitive components in their anti-static packaging until it is time to fit them onto the circuit board. Any MOS device should be supplied in some form of anti-static packing. This is usually conductive foam, ordinary plastic foam with a metal foil covering, a plastic tube, or a blister pack with a metal covering on the backing card. The basic idea is to either insulate the component from static charges, or (more usually) to short circuit all the pins together. This second method does not keep static charges away from the components, but it does ensure that dangerous voltages can not exist from one pin to another. It is a large voltage difference across the pins of a device that can actually cause damage.

Another important precaution is to avoid soldering MOS integrated circuits direct to the component panel. It is much safer if a suitable d.i.l. integrated circuit holder is soldered to the board, and the MOS integrated circuit is then plugged into the holder. It is best to leave out the integrated circuits until a project has been completed in all other respects.

I would strongly urge the use of holders for all integrated circuits, regardless of whether or not they are MOS devices. If you should accidentally fit an integrated circuit the wrong way round, there is little difficulty in gently prising it free from the holder using a small screwdriver, and then fitting it the right way round. Desoldering a multi-pin component from a circuit board can be quite difficult even if you do have access to proper desoldering equipment.

The other main anti-static precaution is to simply avoid getting the devices in contact with any likely sources of high static voltages. For example, when constructing projects avoid wearing clothing made from synthetic fibres. When fitting MOS devices into their holders, try to avoid touching the pins as far as possible. In practice it might be impossible to avoid this completely. You often have to pinch the two rows of pins inwards slightly in order to get the integrated circuits into their holders.

It is essential that integrated circuits are fitted the right way round. Get one of these components the wrong way round, and it could easily be destroyed when the project is switched on. Unfortunately, it is

Figure 1.2 The method of dil ic pin numbering

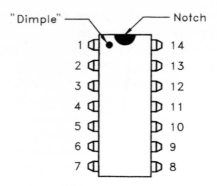

"Dimple" ——— | ——— Notch

probably true to say that, in general, the more expensive the integrated circuit, the more vulnerable it is to damage from this sort of treatment.

To make it easy to get integrated circuits the right way round they have an indentation next to pin 1, plus a U shaped notch at this end of the component. Figure 1.2 shows the notch and the dimple, and as is the convention, the integrated circuit is shown viewed from above. Note that this is the opposite to transistors, which are normally shown as base views in leadout diagrams. It is a 14 pin d.i.l. device that is shown in Figure 1.2, but the same method is used for all normal d.i.l. integrated circuits.

When building projects you do not normally need to worry about the pin numbering. Just get the devices orientated so that the notches and dimples match up with the markings in the component layout diagrams. It is only fair to point out that many integrated circuits seem to have just the notch or only the dimple, but not both. This does not really matter, since either one of them will enable you to get the device orientated correctly. Slightly confusingly, some devices have a sort of notch at the opposite end of the case to the proper one. This is presumably just some sort of moulding mark, and it is not usually difficult to see which is the proper notch and which is not.

The rest

Only three types of socket are used in these projects. The audio inputs and outputs practically all use standard 0.25 inch (6.35 millimetre) jack sockets (see photo 3, page 6). This is probably the most common type of socket in electronic music systems, but it is obviously quite in order to use a different type of connector if it will fit in better with your particular setup. However, if you use a different type, make quite sure that you get it wired-up the right way round. Ordinary open type sockets are shown in the wiring diagrams, and these are the cheapest type.

There are also insulated sockets, which are an enclosed type having a plastic casing. They invariably seem to have some switch contacts that are activated by inserting and removing the jack plug. These contacts are of no use in the current context and simply confuse matters. Any mono jack sockets are usable, but unless you know what you are doing I would recommend the use of the open type, chassis mounting sockets, which have no switch contacts. These require 9.5 millimetre diameter mounting holes incidentally.

One project requires an XLR connector, and another uses a miniature 3.5 millimetre jack sockets. These two components are discussed in the relevant sections of Chapter 2.

Most of the projects use one or more switches, and these are mostly very simple switches. In the components lists I have mainly specified sub-miniature toggle switches (see Photo 3, page 6). A toggle switch is simply one that is controlled via a small lever (known as a 'dolly'). The sub-miniature versions of these switches are extremely small, reasonably cheap, and seem to be quite reliable these days. However, other types of switch, such as slider, rocker and rotary types are also suitable. Bear in mind though, that with these other types of switch the mounting arrangements can be quite awkward. With rocker types in particular, you often have to make a rectangular mounting hole very accurately indeed. Make it just fractionally too small and the switch will not fit into it, or marginally too large and it will not snap into place properly. With the slightest provocation the switch simply drops out the mounting hole.

Sub-miniature toggle switches mostly require a single 6.3 millimetre diameter mounting hole, but the smallest types require 5.2 millimetre diameter mounting holes. Another point to keep in mind is that other types of switch tend to be much larger than sub-miniature toggle types. This can make it difficult to find space for them inside the case, particularly in the case of a small project such as a guitar effects unit.

When dealing with switches you will encounter the terms s.p.s.t., s.p.d.t., d.p.s.t., and d.p.d.t. The first of these stands for single pole single throw, and this is the most simple type of switch. It has just two tags, and it is just a simple on/off type switch. A d.p.s.t. switch is a double pole single throw switch. This is basically just two s.p.s.t. switches controlled by a single lever, slider, or whatever. A switch of this type therefore has four tags. An s.p.d.t. switch is a single pole double throw type. This type of switch has three tags. The centre tag connects to one of the other two, depending on the setting of the lever. These are also known as changeover switches, which is a fair description of their function. A d.p.d.t. switch is a double pole double throw switch, and this is two s.p.d.t. switches controlled in unison. This type of switch therefore has six tags. The components lists make it quite clear which type of switch is required.

A heavy-duty push-button switch is specified for a number of the projects. The point of using a switch of this type is that with the project on the floor it can be operated by foot. This permits a 'look no hands' method to be used when switching guitar effects in and out. Some of the larger component catalogues list one or two heavy-duty push-button switches. Ordinary types can be used, but could well have extremely short operating lives. Heavy-duty push-button switches need quite large mounting holes of about 12.5 millimetres in diameter.

Only one project requires a more complicated type of switch, and this is the 6 way 2 pole rotary switch used in the guitar tuner project. This is a standard form of switch which you should find listed in any electronic components catalogue. The only complication is that you might have the choice of 'break before make' and 'make before break' types. Either type is suitable for the guitar tuner project. Rotary switches normally have 10 millimetre diameter mounting bushes and standard 6 millimetre diameter control shafts.

Batteries

All the projects featured in this book are powered from a 9 volt battery, or possibly two 9 volt batteries. This helps to keep things simple, and for beginners it keeps things safe. The shock from one or two 9 volt batteries is so slight that you are totally unaware of it. The shock from the mains supply can be lethal. For many of the projects a small (PP3 size) battery is adequate, but with some a higher capacity battery is preferable. I would recommend using six HP7 size cells in one of the plastic battery holders that are available from the larger component retailers. The connection to the holder is made via an ordinary PP3 type battery clip incidentally. Other high capacity 9 volt batteries, such as PP9 size batteries, should also be suitable for the projects which have higher current consumptions.

As most readers will be aware, the battery must be connected the right way round. In the early days of semiconductors the likely result of getting the battery connected the wrong way round, even briefly, was the destruction of all the semiconductors in the circuit. Modern semiconductors are mostly more tolerant of the wrong supply voltage, but some integrated circuits will permit very high supply currents to flow if the supply polarity is incorrect. Even if a device should withstand these high currents, it will quickly overheat and be destroyed. Therefore, be very careful to get the battery clip connected with the right polarity. In the wiring diagrams + and − signs are used to indicate the battery polarity. The red battery clip lead is the positive (+) one, and the black lead is the negative (-) one.

Stripboard

These projects are all based on stripboard, which is a form of proprietary printed circuit board (see Photo 4). In some catalogues you may
find it listed under the proprietary name 'Veroboard'. It consists
basically of a piece of thin board which is brown in colour and made
from an insulating material. It is drilled with holes on a 0.1 inch
matrix, and strips of copper join up rows of holes. Figure 1.3 shows
the general scheme of things. Something which tends to confuse some
beginners is that the copper side of the board is often referred to as
the underside, and the non-copper side is called the top side. It might
seem reasonable to assume that the plain side would be called the
underside. However, the components are fitted on the plain side of
the board, which therefore becomes the top side.

   These projects do not use stripboard panels of the standard sizes
in which it is normally sold. Therefore, boards of the correct size
must be cut from larger pieces using a hacksaw. When cutting the
board have the copper side facing upwards. Otherwise the copper
strips that are cut might tend to rip away from the board. Cut along
rows of holes rather than trying to cut between rows (which is virtually impossible as they are so close together). This leaves rather rough
edges, but these can easily be smoothed to a neat finish. Some strip-
boards seem to be made of a rather brittle material that can easily
crack and break when it is being sawn. Always proceed carefully, using
minimal force when cutting.

Photo 4 Stripboard used for
construction of these projects

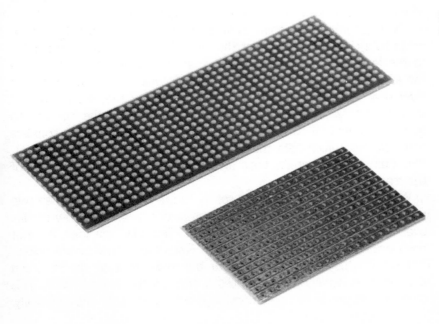

Figure 1.3 Stripboard has holes on a 0.1 in matrix and rows of copper strips

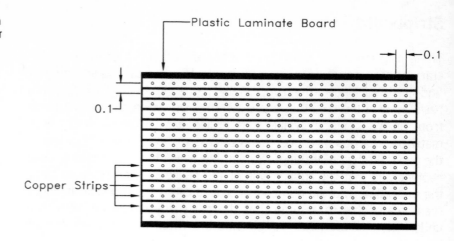

With most projects, some cuts in the copper strips are required. The easiest way to make these is to use the special tool which is available from most suppliers of stripboard. An alternative is to use a 5 mm hand held twist drill. Either way make sure that you cut deep enough to sever the tracks, but not so deep as to seriously weaken the board.

Soldering

The component leads are threaded through the appropriate holes on the non-copper side of the board, and the components are pressed hard against the board. The leads are trimmed on the underside of the board using wire clippers, and then soldered to the copper strips. The leads should be trimmed so that about two or three millimetres of wire protrudes on the underside of the board.

The most important point to keep in mind when soldering components to a circuit board is that the 'bit' of the iron should be applied to the joint first, and then some solder should be fed in. This gets the joint hot before the solder is applied, which helps the solder to flow over the joint properly. What is definitely the wrong way of tackling this type of joint is to put some solder onto the iron and to then try to apply it to the lead and copper strip. The solder contains cores of flux which help the solder to flow properly over the joint. This flux tends to rapidly burn away if solder is placed on the bit of the iron.

When you try to transfer the solder to the joint there are then two problems. Firstly, with little flux in the solder it will not flow readily over the leadout wire and copper strip. Secondly, the joint has not been pre-heated, which also tends to restrict the flow of the solder. The result is usually a reluctance for the solder to leave the iron, and if it does, it usually just produces a blob on the leadout wire. This gives a joint which is highly unreliable both electrically and physically.

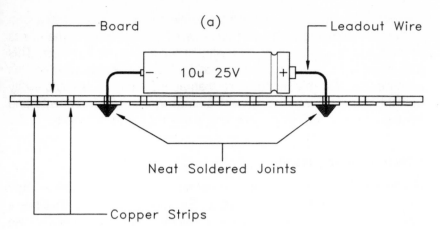

Figure 1.4 A good soldered joint has a mountain shape, as in (a). The blob shape of (b) usually means that a 'dry' joint has been produced

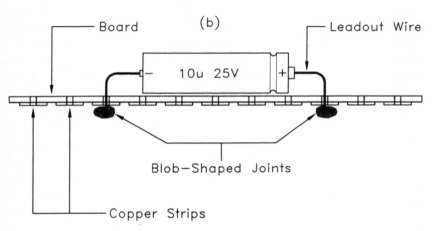

Although this may seem to be an easy way of soldering, it is very ineffective and should definitely not be used.

Although you should not try to solder in this way, you should place some solder onto the bit of the iron from time to time, so as to always keep the end nicely covered with some reasonably fresh solder. This is known as 'tinning' the bit. The point of doing this is that it helps to give a good thermal contact between the bit and the joints, which helps to give good quality results, as in Figure 1.4(a).

If you end up with a blob shaped joint, as in Figure 1.4(b), then it is likely that you have a 'dry' joint which is not making a proper electrical connection between the lead and the copper strip. Other tell-tale signs of a bad joint are lots of burnt flux around the joint, and a dull, crazed appearance to the solder instead of the normal shiny finish. If you end up with a suspect joint, it is best to remove the solder, clean up the end of the leadout wire and the copper strip around it using a small file, and then try again.

I would strongly urge newcomers to electronic project construction to practise soldering on a small piece of stripboard using some pieces of wire and resistors, prior to trying to build their first project. This may seem a bit wasteful, but the cost of the materials used in this exercise will probably be no more than about a pound. It could easily prevent you from wasting several pounds worth of components and a lot of time on a first project which becomes a total failure.

Which soldering iron?

It is important to use a suitable soldering iron and type of solder. Any small electric iron should be suitable. By small I mean one that has a rating of somewhere around 15 to 25 watts. There is no need to use something elaborate such as a temperature controlled iron. An ordinary 'no frills' iron will do the job perfectly well. A matching soldering iron stand should be considered essential, not an optional extra. For modern electronic work a small bit is required. One of around 2 to 2.5 millimetres in diameter should be suitable. Trying to solder components onto stripboard using an iron fitted with a bit much larger than this can be very difficult indeed. You are likely to find that you have soldered each lead to two or three copper strips!

The solder should be a multi-cored type intended for electrical and electronic work. It is generally available in two thicknesses. The 22 s.w.g. type is the thinner gauge, and is the most useful for building circuit boards. The much thicker 18 s.w.g. solder is better for larger joints, such as when wiring up the controls and sockets. I would not recommend the 18 s.w.g. type for building circuit boards. If you are going to buy only one gauge of solder, then the 22 s.w.g. type is definitely the one to buy. However, it is useful to buy a small amount of the 18 s.w.g. type as well.

Missing links

If you look at the diagrams which show the component sides of the circuit boards, you will notice that there are numerous pairs of holes joined by lines. These lines represent link wires, which are unavoidable when using stripboard with modern components. These wires can in most cases be made from the pieces of wire trimmed from resistor leadout wires. I do not suggest this method of working just as an economy measure - the wire used for most resistor leadouts is ideal for use as link wires.

In some cases too many link wires might be needed, or some of the wires might be longer than the available leadout trimmings. The link wires must then be made from some 22 or 24 s.w.g. tinned copper wire. 22 s.w.g. is a bit thicker than is ideal, and 24 s.w.g. is slightly thinner than would be ideal. I find that 24 s.w.g. wire is slightly easier to use than 22 s.w.g. wire, but this is just a personal preference.

It is important that the link wires are quite taut, as there is otherwise a risk of short circuits occurring. I find the best way of fitting them is to first solder one end of the link in place. Then thread the other end of the wire through the appropriate hole in the board, pull it tight using some pliers, trim it to length on the underside of the board, and then solder it in place. If you want to make absolutely certain that no short circuits to any link wires occur, simply fit pieces of p.v.c. sleeving over them. However, I have never found it necessary to do this provided the link wires are made reasonably taut.

Wiring-up

In most projects there is a certain amount of wiring from the circuit board to off-board components, such as switches, sockets, potentiometers, etc. There may also be some wiring from one off-board component to another. This is generally known by such names as 'hard wiring', 'spaghetti wiring', and 'point-to-point wiring'. Whatever your preferred term, it is normally completed using thin multi-strand wire. Something like 7/0.2 (i.e. seven cores of 0.2 millimetre diameter wire), p.v.c. insulated wire is suitable. This, or something similar, should be found in any electronics component catalogue. It will probably be described as 'hook- up' wire or 'connecting' wire. Single core wire, which is also known as solid core wire, is less than ideal for most hard wiring. It is not very flexible, and unless used very carefully it has a tendency to break.

I often use ribbon cable for wiring up projects. Ribbon cable is a multi-way cable that consists of what are effectively several pieces of multi-strand p.v.c. insulated connecting wire laid side-by-side. The wires are fixed together by an overall covering of transparent plastic. It lives up to its name as this type of cable is flat and ribbon-like. It is available as a single coloured (usually grey) cable, or as multi-coloured 'rainbow' cable. The latter is better for wiring-up purposes as having each lead a different colour makes it easy to tell which lead is which. This cable is available from 10 way to about 50 way cable. For our present purposes any ribbon cable will do, but ten way cable is probably the most practical choice.

Usually when you are wiring-up a project you will find that there is not a single wire running from the component panel to an off-board component. In most cases there are two, three or four leads running from the circuit board to each off-board component. There would normally be three leads in the case of a potentiometer for example.

In order to help keep things as neat as possible, the circuit boards are designed so that, as far as reasonably possible, all the leads that go to an off-board component emanate from the same area of the board.

When wiring-up a project using ordinary hook-up wire you can make things neater by tying together the wires in each group. Ribbon cable represents an easier way of obtaining the same effect. If you have three leads running from the board to an off-board component, first break away a three way cable from the main piece of ribbon cable, and then cut off a suitable length. This can then be used to provide the three connections to the off-board component. No cable tying is required, as the leads are already held together as a single cable.

A small piece of insulation must be removed from the end of each lead before it can be connected to the tag of an off-board component. It is important to use a pair of wire strippers to do this. You can remove the insulation using scissors, a penknife, etc., but you could easily end up injuring yourself. Also, you are likely to damage the wire, which will then fatigue easily, and is likely to snap before too long. Wire strippers enable the insulation to be removed quickly and easily, and they can be adjusted so that they will cut just the right depth into the insulation, leaving the wires unharmed.

Off-board components

Making connections to off-board components requires a slightly different method of soldering to the one described previously. First, it is important to tin the ends of the leads and the tags of the components with a generous amount of solder. In most cases you will find that the leads and tags take the solder without any difficulty, but some may not. This will be due to dirt or corrosion, which can be scraped away using a miniature file or the blade of a small penknife. Once the tinning has been completed, hook the end of the lead through and around the hole in the appropriate component tag. Then apply the iron and some solder in the normal way, and a good strong joint should be produced. Some component tags are actually pins which lack the hole. With these you simply hook the wire around the pin, and then solder it in place in the normal way.

Solder pins

At the component panel end of the hard wiring you could connect the leads direct to the stripboard. This tends to be a rather awkward way of going about matters, and is also unreliable. The wires tend to break away from the board the pieces of strip to which they are connected.

A better way of tackling things is to use solder pins at the points on the board where connections to off-board components must be made. For 0.1 inch stripboard it is the 1 millimetre diameter pins that are required. There are single and double sided pins, but for the projects featured here you will probably only need the single sided type. These are inserted from the copper side of the board, and pushed home so that very little is left protruding on the underside of the board. A tool for fitting solder pins is available, but they can usually be pushed into place properly with the aid of some pliers. Use a generous amount of solder when connecting the pins to the copper strips, and also tin the tops of the pins with liberal amount of solder. There should then be no difficulty in connecting the leads to them

Boxing clever

There is a vast range of project cases available these days, from inexpensive plastic boxes through to elaborate metal instrument cases which, if used for most projects, would account for more than 50% of the overall cost. There is no one case which is suitable for all the projects in this book. The projects cover various types and complexities, and whereas a cheap plastic box might be appropriate to one project, another might require a larger metal case. Where appropriate, the text gives some guidance as to the best type and size of case for each project. The size of the component panel will give you a good idea of the minimum size of case that is needed.

Mounting tension

There are three basic methods of mounting completed component panels inside cases. The most simple is to mount the board in the guide rails that are moulded into many plastic cases, and a few aluminium types. This is only possible if the board is made to a size that will fit into the guide rails with a fair degree of precision. This method is not applicable to most of the projects featured here, although it might be possible in some instances if the board is made larger than is really necessary, so that it will fit the guide rails properly.

My preferred method is to simply bolt the board in place using 6BA nuts and bolts. If your supplier sells only metric sizes, M3 is the nearest metric equivalent to 6BA. Whichever of these you use, 3.3 millimetre diameter mounting holes are suitable. It is important to use spacers about 5 to 10 millimetres long over the mounting bolts, between the case and the component panel. Alternatively, some extra nuts can be used as spacers. If you are using a metal case these will hold the connections on the underside of the board clear of the metal case, so that they do not short circuit through it.

Whatever type of case you use, the spacers will prevent the board from buckling slightly as the mounting nuts are tightened. This buckling occurs because the underside of the board is far from flat once the components have been added, and there are soldered joints protruding on the underside of the board. If you omit the spacers, it is quite possible that the board will buckle so badly that it will crack, or even break into several pieces.

The final method is to use the special plastic stand-offs that are available from most electronic component retailers. These vary somewhat in design, but the most simple type clip into the case and then the board is clipped onto them. The holes in the case and the board must be drilled very accurately if this type of stand-off is to work properly. With the stand-offs of this type that I have used, they never really seemed to hold the board in place properly. There is an alternative type which is mounted on the case via self-tapping screws, and these seem to be more reliable. However, with stripboard I much prefer to have the component panels securely bolted to the case.

Layout

When designing the overall layout of a project you need to give some thought to how the unit will be used. For instance, do not have sockets too close to, or immediately above control knobs. It is very easy to produce a front panel layout that looks very neat and plausible, but when you plug in the input and output leads the plugs get in the way and make it virtually impossible to adjust some of the controls.

In general it is best to keep inputs well separated from outputs. This is more important with some projects than with others. In the worst cases, having an input socket anywhere near to the output socket is almost certain to render the circuit unstable, possibly preventing it from working at all. Where the layout of a project is critical in this way, or in any other manner, this is pointed out in the text. Try to avoid layouts that result in lots of crossed-over wires when you wire-up the project. This is not just a matter of making the interior of the project look neat. Long leads trailing all over the place can reduce the performance of a circuit or cause instability. Also, if there should be a problem with the project at some time, fault finding will be much easier if the wiring is neat, tidy and easy to follow.

The right order

This covers the basics of project construction, and should tell you most of what you need to know. The rest can be learned from looking through one or two large component catalogues, and from experience. A summary of the basic steps in building a project is provided below. This list has the steps in the order that I would suggest you go about things. Not everyone would totally agree with this, and you might prefer to do things your own way in due course, but this gives you a sound initial method of working.

Step by step project building

1. Order all the components you need, being careful to get the right ones (including the right types of capacitor etc.).
2. Once you have all the components, identify them all, and check that you have been supplied with the correct parts.
3. Cut the stripboard to size, make the breaks in the copper strips and drill the mounting holes.
4. Fit the components and link wires to the board. Start at one end and work your way methodically to the other side of the board. Fit the solder pins, but do not put the integrated circuits in their holders yet.
5. Work out the case layout, and drill all the holes.
6. Fit the controls and sockets in the case, and then fit the component panel.
7. Wire-up the project using hook-up wire or pieces of ribbon cable.
8. Fit the integrated circuits in their holders.
9. Check the wiring etc., and when all is well, switch on and test the project.

Testing

If a project fails to work, and you do not have the necessary technical skills and equipment to check it properly, all is not lost. The problem could be due to a faulty component, but in all honesty this is highly unlikely provided you buy new components from any respectable supplier. There are many 'bargain packs' of components on offer, and some of these represent outstanding value for money. Others, with the best will in the world, have to be regarded as bags of rubbish. Without technical expertise and some test equipment it is not possible to sort out the good from the bad. Therefore, it is advisable for beginners to use only new components of good quality.

Faulty components

Even if you use top quality components from one of the larger retailers it is obviously still possible that a faulty component could slip through. This is extremely rare though, since components undergo quite stringent testing. Where a faulty component is supplied it is usually due to it having sustained physical damage somewhere along the line. This damage, such as a missing leadout wire, will almost invariably be obvious when you examine the newly obtained components. At one time there were companies selling semiconductors of dubious quality. Some of these were not quite what they purported to be, while others were so-called 'genuine duds' that failed to work at all. Fortunately, this practice seemed to die out some years ago. Any semiconductors you buy will almost certainly be the real thing from one of the main semiconductor manufacturers.

Problems are unlikely to be due to faulty components, but it is a good idea to inspect the board visually for signs of damaged components. Are there any discoloured components which overheated when you took too long to solder them into circuit? Are there other signs of damage, such as a polyester capacitor that is parting company with one of its leadout wires? Replace any suspect looking components.

Wrong components

The wrong component rather than a faulty component is a much more likely cause of problems. Check the circuit board carefully against the diagrams and components list, making sure that the right parts are in the right places.

Faulty construction

With stripboard construction you need to be very careful not to get one or two or the leadout wires connected to the wrong copper strip. Are the electrolytic capacitors and semiconductors fitted the right way round? You are unlikely to miss out a component, as you would presumably notice that there was one left over. Link wires are a different matter though. Check that there are the same number of link wires on the component layout diagram and on the circuit board.

Dry joints

Probably the most likely area for faults is on the underside of the board. Did you place the solder on the bit of the iron and then transfer it to the joint? This virtually guarantees bad joints, but is the method that many beginners seem to insist on adopting. If there are any suspect joints, remove the solder from them, clean up the copper strip and leadout wire by scraping then with the blade of a penknife, and try again using the correct method of soldering (as described previously in this chapter). When inspecting the underside of the board look out for joints that are globular in appearance, solder that has a dull rather than a shiny surface, and joints that are covered with burned and black flux. These often mean that the joint concerned is something less than perfect.

Copper strip breaks ok?

Another point to check is that the breaks in the copper strips are all present and in the right places. If you find that a break has been made in the wrong place, simply solder a piece of wire over the break and make a new one in the right place. Look carefully at each break to determine whether or not it has been fully cut though. On several occasions I have found that a newly constructed project has failed to work due to a minute trail of copper bridging what should be a break in a copper strip. These are sometimes so thin that they are barely visible with the naked eye. A magnifying glass is more than slightly helpful when inspecting the underside of a stripboard.

With stripboard construction the main cause of faults is short circuits between adjacent copper strips due to minute blobs of excess solder. The copper strips are so close together that it is very easy to solder across two strips. This will often be quite obvious, as the strips will be bridged over a length of several millimetres. Sometimes though, there may be only a very fine trail of solder which is barely visible. Once again, a magnifying glass is very helpful when making a visual inspection of the copper side of the board. Even with an aid to vision, some solder trails can be very difficult to locate. Cleaning the underside of the board with one of the special cleaners that are available can help matters. Look especially carefully at areas of the board where there are a lot of soldered joints.

A technique which I have found quite useful is to carefully score between each pair of copper strips using a sharp modelling knife. If there are any solder trails which are so small that they are defeating your eyesight, this treatment should cut through them and remove the problem. Some years ago when I was making large numbers of projects on stripboard I found that this method was successful in curing a surprisingly large percentage of ailing circuit boards.

2 Guitar projects

Do-it-yourself projects for use with guitars have been very popular for many years now. It is an area of electronic project construction where you can still build useful devices that will usually cost much less than ready-made alternatives. You can also produce interesting and useful projects that have no ready-made equivalents.

Guitar preamplifier

It is amazing just how different the output characteristics of guitar pick-ups can be. Good quality modern pick-ups seem to achieve an output level of around one volt peak to peak from a medium source imped-ance. This signal level, incidentally, is the one achieved just after the initial signal peak, and is not an optimistic one based on the peak level from the pick-up. Inexpensive and some older guitar pick-ups often have very much lower output levels. I have a couple of guitar pick-ups which seem to achieve an output of only about 100 millivolts r.m.s. initially, and after the initial 'twang' the signal level decays fairly rapidly. The home-made pick-ups that were popular about 15 to 25 years ago have even lower output levels, but from a very low source impedance.

If you have a guitar fitted with high output pick-ups you will proba-bly find that it operates perfectly well with practically any amplifier, mixer, effects unit, or whatever. With low output types the situation is more difficult, and the guitar may fail to drive some units properly. Many amplifiers for instance, lack any inputs with sufficient sensitiv-ity for a low output pick-up. Most guitar effects units are designed to accommodate high level signals, low level signals, or anything in-between. However, even with these you can occasionally run into diffi-culties. With effects units that are not specifically designed for operation with electric guitars, results are often very disappointing if they are used with low output pick-ups.

Circuit operation

There is a simple solution to this problem in the form of a guitar preamplifier. This simply boosts the output from a low output pick-up to a level that can reliably drive virtually any amplifier, effects unit,

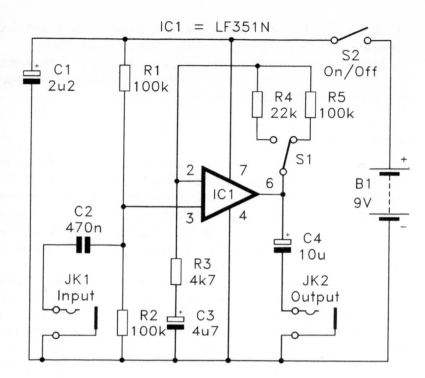

IC1 = LF351N

Figure 2.1 The guitar preamplifier circuit diagram. S1 enables one of two gain levels to be selected

etc. Figure 2.1 shows the circuit diagram for a guitar preamplifier which offers two levels of voltage gain. The circuit is basically just a standard operational amplifier non-inverting mode type. R1 and R2 bias the input of the amplifier, and set the input impedance at about 50k. This should give good results with almost any guitar pick-up.

The voltage gain of the circuit is determined by the two resistors in the negative feedback network. These resistors are either R3 and R4, or R3 and R5, depending on the setting of S1. If we first consider the circuit with R4 connected into circuit, the voltage gain of the amplifier is equal to (R3 + R4) divided by R3. This works out at a voltage gain of about 5.7 times. This setting should be used when only a modest boost to the signal level is required. With R5 switched into circuit the voltage gain formula becomes (R3 + R5) divided by R3, which gives a gain figure of about 22 times. This should be sufficient to boost the output from even very low output pick-ups to the point where they can drive most amplifiers etc. properly. However, if necessary the gain can be boosted somewhat by making R5 a little higher in value (about 180k).

IC1 is an inexpensive bifet device which gives good performance in audio applications. It would be possible to use an expensive ultra-low noise operational amplifier for IC1 in order to obtain better performance, but in practice this would probably not be worthwhile. Although an LF351N is specified for IC1, similar operational amplifiers such as the TLO71CP and TLO81CP are also suitable. This is also true where the LF351N is specified for other projects in this book.

The current consumption of the circuit is only about 2 milliamps. This is low enough to give a very long battery life from a low capacity (PP3 size) 9 volt battery.

Construction

Figure 2.2 shows the component layout for the stripboard panel, while Figure 2.3 shows the underside (copper side) of the board. The arrowheads at the corner of the board show how the board has been turned over. The hard wiring is shown in Figure 2.4 (which should be used in conjunction with Figure 2.2). A board having 24 holes by 16 copper strips is required. The principles of stripboard construction are covered in detail in Chapter 1.

For an audio project such as this there is some advantage in using a case of all metal construction. This will be earthed to the negative supply rail via the input and output sockets, and it will tend to screen the wiring from stray pick up of mains 'hum' and other electrical noise. Diecast aluminium boxes are popular for guitar projects as they have excellent screening properties, and are also extremely tough. However, satisfactory results will probably be obtained using an inexpensive plastic box provided you are careful not to position the interface very near to any powerful sources of electrical interference (mains cables, transformers in power amplifiers, etc.). Virtually any small plastic or metal box should accommodate all the parts.

Figure 2.2 The guitar preamplifier stripboard layout. The board has 24 holes by 16 copper strips

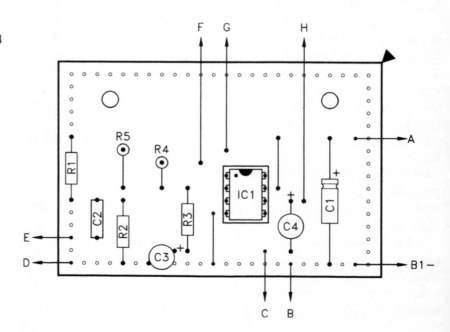

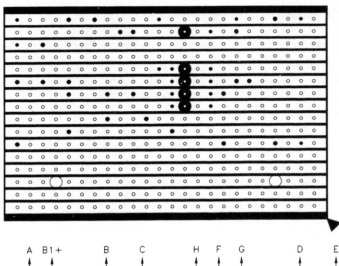

Figure 2.3 The underside of the guitar preamp board

S2   JK2   S1   JK1

Figure 2.4 The hard wiring in the guitar preamplifier

User tips

In use, the preamplifier is simply connected between the guitar and the guitar amplifier. The existing guitar lead can be used to connect the guitar to the preamplifier, but an extra lead will be needed to connect the preamplifier to the power amplifier (or mixer, etc.). Both leads must be good quality screened types in order to minimise any stray pick up of 'hum' and other electrical noise.

Components (Guitar preamplifier)

Resistors
(all 0.25 watt 5% carbon film)
R1   100k   R4   22k
R2   100k   R5   100k
R3   4k7   2x 1·68

Capacitors
C1   2u2 10V axial elect   0·13
C2   470n polyester   0·25
C3   4u7 10V radial elect   0·10
C4   10u 10V radial elect   0·10

Semiconductor
IC1   LF351N   0·38

Miscellaneous
JK1   Standard jack socket   0·33 x2
JK2   Standard jack socket
S1   s.p.d.t. min toggle   0·73 x2 — 1·46
S2   s.p.s.t. min toggle
B1   9 volt (PP3 size)
      0.1 inch stripboard 24 holes   1·09
      by 16 strips
      Small metal or plastic case   1·66
      Battery connector   0·10
      8 pin d.i.l. i.c. holder   0·06
      Wire, solder, etc.   1·23   £12·26

Headphone amplifier

It would be nice to think that everyone within hearing distance appreciates our efforts when we are practising new pieces, or honing some of our existing repertoire to perfection. Unfortunately, not everyone is going to share our taste in music, our playing may not always be that good, and few pieces of music sound good when heard for the nth time this week! For users of electronic instruments there is an easy solution in the form of headphones. The same approach is possible with guitars as well, and most power amplifiers have a headphone socket. But if you want to practise without an amp, there is an alternative in the form of a guitar headphone amplifier, such as the unit described here. This is a small, battery powered, Walkman™ type device, which enables you to practise practically anywhere without disturbing others.

This headphone amplifier is based on a small audio power amplifier integrated circuit. This means that it has plenty of drive, so that it can drive even low sensitivity headphones at good volume. About the only kind of headphones it will not drive properly are the ones that are designed to be fed from the loudspeaker outputs of large power amplifiers. Headphones of this type are something of a rarity, so this is not a significant limitation. The output of the unit is actually too great for most headphones, and it must be limited somewhat in order to avoid any risk to the health of your hearing and the headphones. The power amplifier integrated circuit has plenty of gain, so it gives good results with low output guitar pick-ups. The gain may be excessive for many guitar pick-ups, but a very simple modification is all that is needed in order to reduce the gain to a more suitable level.

Circuit operation

Figure 2.5 shows the circuit diagram for the guitar headphone amplifier. The unit is based on IC1, which is an LM386N low voltage audio power amplifier. In common with most other modern integrated circuit power amplifiers, this one can have its input direct coupled to the volume control potentiometer (VR1). There are actually two inputs, a non-inverting one at pin 3, and an inverting one at pin 2. In this circuit the inverting input is left unused, and is tied to the negative supply rail in order to avoid stray pick up. Due to the use of direct coupling at the input, it is a important that no d.c. component is present on the input signal. With a guitar pick-up the input signal should be a purely a.c. type, but this is a point that should be borne in mind if you should try to use the unit with any other signal source.

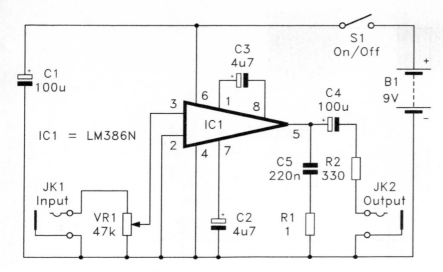

Figure 2.5 The guitar headphone amplifier circuit diagram. C3 is not needed for use with high output pick-ups

The voltage gain of the amplifier is controlled by an internal negative feedback circuit. The only discrete component required to complete this network is d.c. blocking capacitor C3. With high output pick-ups the full voltage gain of the circuit will not be needed. It is advisable to reduce the gain of the circuit if the unit is used with a high output pick-up, or adjustment of the volume control could be very tricky. Advancing it just a few degrees from zero would produce maximum volume. The gain can be reduced by adding a resistor in series with C3, but simply removing C3 altogether should give a suitable voltage gain.

C1 is a supply decoupling capacitor which helps to avoid instability due to feedback through the supply lines. C2 decouples the supply to the preamplifier stage of IC1. C5 and R1 form what is sometimes called a Zobel network, and these also aid good stability. C4 provides d.c. blocking at the output, and R2 attenuates the output signal to a suitable level for most headphones. However, if the unit lacks drive R2 can be reduced in value, or it the amplifier is capable of providing excess output levels, R2 can be made higher in value.

The current consumption of the circuit is approximately 4 milliamps, although this might rise slightly at high volume levels using insensitive headphones. Even so, a PP3 size 9 volt battery is perfectly adequate as the power source.

Construction

Details of the stripboard component layout, breaks in the copper strips, and point-to-point wiring are provided in Figures 2.6, 2.7, and 2.8 respectively. The board has 25 holes by 16 copper strips.

Figure 2.6 The component layout for the headphone amplifier. The board has 25 holes by 16 strips

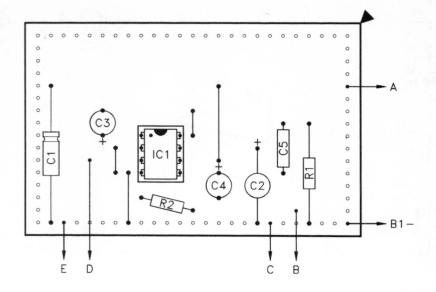

Figure 2.7 The underside of the headphone amplifier board

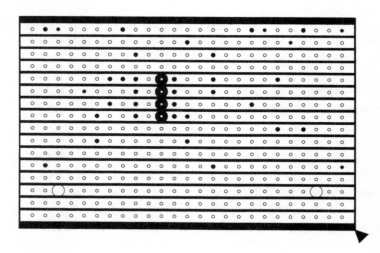

Figure 2.8 The headphone amplifier point-to-point wiring

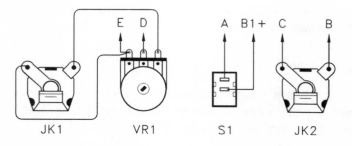

It has been assumed in Figure 2.8 that JK2 is a standard (mono) jack socket. If you are using the unit with stereo headphones, then a standard stereo jack socket should be used for JK2. Results will almost certainly be best with the two phones wired in series. This is achieved by connecting the two wires from the component panel to the outer two tags of the socket. Leave the middle (chassis) tag unconnected. For this method to work properly it is important that there is no connection from the chassis of JK1 to the chassis of JK2 through the metal case. You could insulate JK1 and (or) JK2 from the case, but it is much easier to use a plastic case for this project.

User tip

The unit is connected to the guitar via an ordinary screened jack lead, although it might be worth while making up a short jack lead specifically for use with the headphone amplifier.

Components (Headphone amplifier)

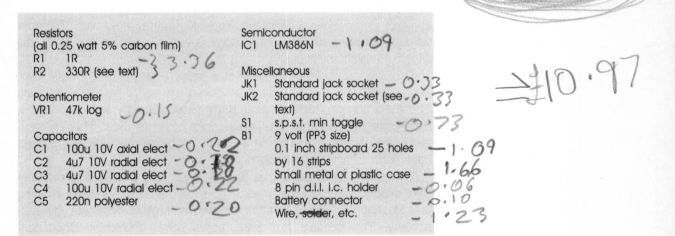

Resistors (all 0.25 watt 5% carbon film)	Semiconductor	
R1 1R	IC1 LM386N	— 1·09
R2 330R (see text)		
	Miscellaneous	
	JK1 Standard jack socket	— 0·33
Potentiometer	JK2 Standard jack socket (see	— 0·33
VR1 47k log ~0·15	text)	
	S1 s.p.s.t. min toggle	— 0·73
Capacitors	B1 9 volt (PP3 size)	
C1 100u 10V axial elect ~0·22	0.1 inch stripboard 25 holes	— 1·09
C2 4u7 10V radial elect — 0·18	by 16 strips	
C3 4u7 10V radial elect — 0·22	Small metal or plastic case	— 1·66
C4 100u 10V radial elect — 0·22	8 pin d.i.l. i.c. holder	— 0·06
C5 220n polyester — 0·20	Battery connector	— 0·10
	Wire, solder, etc.	— 1·23

Resistors: 3 3·36

£10·97

Soft distortion unit

Distortion or 'fuzz' effect units must have been around for almost as long as electric guitars themselves. This is a very simple effect to produce, but some distortion units are very much more musical than others. Many of the published designs for distortion units produce hard clipping, which gives a very harsh sound. Figure 2.9(a) helps to explain what is meant by hard clipping. Here a sinewave signal is clipped symmetrically, and clipping simply means that the signal is not

Figure 2.9 Hard clipping (a) produces a harsh effect, while soft clipping (b) gives a thicker sound

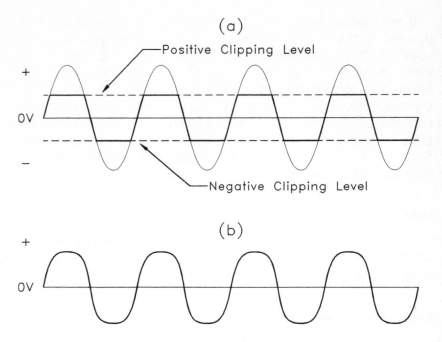

allowed to go above a certain voltage. No matter how high the input voltage becomes, the output voltage is not allowed to go above the clipping threshold level.

This is basically what happens if a modern amplifier is overloaded, and a hard clipping fuzz unit produces the same severe distortion. The distortion products generated are predominantly at high frequencies, giving a bright effect, which does have its uses. This effect is considered to be too extreme by many guitarists though, and it does have some practical limitations.

The worst of these is that it generates very strong intermodulation products. What this means to someone using a hard clipping unit is that they must not permit two strings to resonate simultaneously. The penalty for doing so is some extremely discordant sounds! This effect also tends to be rather uncontrollable. It is easy to have a massive amount of distortion or none at all, but anything in between is virtually impossible. This is simply because even a small amount of hard clipping tends to produce very strong distortion products.

There is an alternative to hard clipping in the form of soft clipping. Figure 2.9(b) shows the sort of waveform that is produced if a sinewave is subjected to soft clipping. This effect is produced by not having a well defined clipping level. In fact there is no true clipping level at all. Instead, as the input voltage increases, the gain of the circuit decreases. Rather than simply clipping off the tops of waveforms, the signals are rounded down.

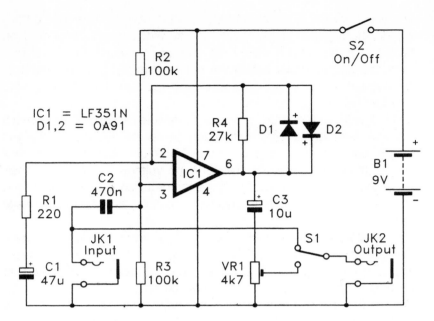

Figure 2.10 The distortion unit circuit diagram

As far as the sound of the effect is concerned, soft clipping is far less harsh. Not only are the distortion products less strong, they also have a much weaker high frequency content. This gives a much 'thicker' effect, and one which most people find very much more musical than the hard clipping sound. Also, it gives much weaker intermodulation distortion. This gives acceptable results when playing more than one string at a time.

Circuit operation

Figure 2.10 shows the circuit diagram for the soft distortion unit. This is basically just an operational amplifier non-inverting mode circuit having a voltage gain of over 100. It differs from the standard non-inverting amplifier configuration in that D1 and D2 are included in the negative feedback circuit. One diode processes positive half cycles, and the other processes negative half cycles. On suitably strong positive going half cycles D1 is brought into conduction, and it shunts R4. D2 has the same effect on negative going output signals. When conductive the diodes reduce the gain of the amplifier.

Silicon diodes have well defined forward conduction threshold voltages, and they start to conduct at a voltage of around 0.6 volts. A voltage only slightly higher than the conduction threshold voltage is sufficient to produce a large current flow. When used in a circuit such as this the result is that the output signal is hard clipped at about plus and minus 0.6 volts. Any signal that tries to take the output outside these limits simply results in the diodes conducting hard on the signal peaks, and reducing the gain of the circuit to a level that keeps the output signal within the plus and minus 0.6 volt limits. If you require a unit which produces hard clipping, use silicon diodes such as 1N4148s for D1 and D2.

The specified diodes are germanium devices, and these have much less well defined forward conduction threshold voltages. They will actually conduct at quite low forward voltages, but they will have quite a high resistance. As the forward voltage is increased, their resistance steadily reduces. This gives the required soft clipping effect, with the gain of the amplifier steadily decreasing as the output voltage rises.

S1 enables the effect to be switched out when it is not required. The output level from IC1 is likely to be higher than the direct output from the guitar. Therefore, VR1 has been included so that the output of the circuit can be reduced to a level that is comparable to that from the guitar pick-up. Adjustment of VR1 has to be a subjective matter, since the output signal is at an almost constant level during the course of each note. By contrast, the output from the guitar pick-up will start at a high level, and substantially decay during each note. It is therefore a matter of giving VR1 a setting that gives no obvious change in volume as the effect is switched in and out.

R4 has been given a value that is suitable for low output guitar pick-ups. If the unit is fed from high output pick-ups it would be better to use a much lower value. About 2k7 should be suitable. You can vary the strength of the effect by altering the value of R4. High values give a stronger effect – lower values give a weaker effect.

The current consumption of the circuit is only about 2 milliamps. A PP3 size 9 volt battery is adequate as the power source, and each battery should give over one hundred hours of operation.

Construction

Details of the stripboard panel are provided in Figure 2.11 and 2.12, while Figure 2.13 shows the point-to-point wiring. The board has 19 holes by 16 copper strips. Construction of the unit is very straightforward, and offers little out of the ordinary. Remember that D1 and D2 are germanium diodes, and that they are more vulnerable to heat damage than are ordinary silicon diodes. Ideally S1 should be a heavy duty push-button switch so that it can be operated by foot. An s.p.s.t. switch of this type might be difficult to obtain, but a d.p.d.t. type is suitable. Simply use one set of three tags, and just ignore the other set.

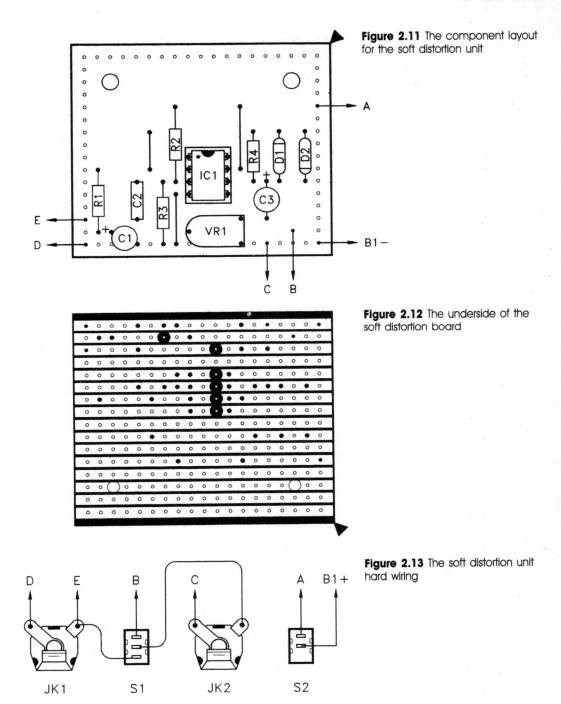

Figure 2.11 The component layout for the soft distortion unit

Figure 2.12 The underside of the soft distortion board

Figure 2.13 The soft distortion unit hard wiring

User tip

In use it should be borne in mind that the unit adds some extra gain to the system. This means that extra care is needed in order to avoid problems with feedback, 'hum' pick-up, etc.

41

Components (Soft distortion unit)

Resistors		**Miscellaneous**	
(all 0.25 watt 5% carbon film)		JK1 Standard jack socket	*O ·23*
R1 220R		JK2 Standard jack socket	*O ·33*
R2 100k	*3×1·68*	S1 s.p.d.t. heavy duty push-	*2·51*
R3 100k		button	
R4 27k (see text)	*=5·04*	S2 s.p.s.t. min toggle —	*O·73*
		B1 9 volt (PP3 size)	
Potentiometer		0.1 inch stripboard 19 holes	*1·0*
VR1 4k7 min hor preset	*0·15*	by 16 strips	
		Small metal or plastic case	*1·6*
Capacitors		8 pin d.i.l. i.c. holder	*O·06*
C1 47u 10V radial elect	*0·10*	Battery connector	*O·10*
C2 470n polyester	*0·25*	Wire, solder, etc.	*1·23*
C3 10u 10V radial elect	*0·10*		
Semiconductors			*~£14·36*
IC1 LF351N	*0·38*		
D1 OA90 or OA91	*0·15*		
D2 OA90 or OA91	*0·15*		

Compressor

Compression is one of the more subtle guitar effects, and it merely changes the envelope of the sound. In other words, it alters the changes in volume that occur during the course of each note. The basic affect of compression is to largely remove these changes. The 'twangy' sound of a guitar is caused by its high initial volume, followed by a fairly rapid decay in level. By removing the initial transient, and giving a more consistent level thereafter, a compression unit gives a sound that is not particularly twangy in character. In fact it is usually rather organ-like with most guitars.

It should perhaps be pointed out that this effect used to be called the 'sustain' effect (and may still be known to some readers by this name). This name is derived from the elongated sustain period that is possible using this effect. Of course, the signal can not be sustained indefinitely, as it will eventually fall to such a low level that it would require an impractically large amount of gain in order to maintain it at the full volume level. With most guitars a sustain period of a few seconds is possible on all but the highest notes.

Circuit operation

Figure 2.14 shows the full circuit diagram for the compression effect unit. IC1 is used as a simple buffer stage at the input of the unit.

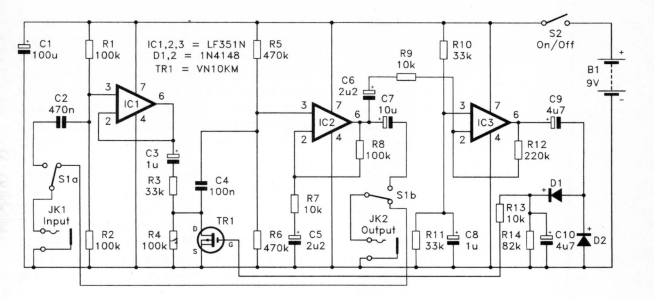

Figure 2.14 The compressor circuit diagram. TR1 is a VMOS transistor

The output from IC1 is coupled to a simple v.c.a. (voltage controlled attenuator) based on TR1. This is an unusual type of transistor – an N channel VMOS device. In this circuit it operates as a sort of voltage controlled resistor. With a gate voltage of about one volt or less it has an extremely high drain to source resistance. Raising the gate voltage above one volt results in this resistance falling considerably. In fact it will be just a few ohms with the gate forward biased by a few volts. With TR1 cutoff there are only small losses through R3, but with it biased hard into conduction, the losses are massive. In fact the control range of the v.c.a. is much larger than would ever be needed in this application.

IC2 operates as a non-inverting amplifier having a voltage gain of just over 20dB (ten times). This gain is needed because the basic action of the unit is to let high level signals pass more or less unaltered, but to boost lower level signals up to the same amplitude as the high level ones. Obviously some voltage gain is needed in order to do this, and the higher the voltage gain, the greater the amount of sustain that can be obtained. In reality there is a limit on the amount of sustain that can be used. Using more than about 20dB of gain could easily result in problems with hum pick up, excessive background hiss, and feedback.

Some of the output of IC3 is fed to an inverting amplifier based on IC3. This has a gain of about 26dB (twenty times). Its output is coupled to a rectifier and smoothing circuit based on D1 and D2. This circuit generates a positive voltage across R14 that is roughly proportional to the strength of the input signal. This voltage is used as the control signal for the v.c.a.

The rectifier and smoothing circuit has a fast attack time, and at the beginning of each note it quickly produces a strong control signal that gives large losses through the v.c.a. The decay time of the circuit is much longer, but is still fairly short in absolute terms. Therefore, as the signal level dies away on each note, so does the control voltage to the v.c.a. This gives a reduction in the losses through the v.c.a., and maintains an almost constant output level until a note is allowed to decay to such a low level that it can no longer be properly sustained.

S1 enables the effect to be switched out, and it does so by simply bypassing the compression circuit unit altogether. The value of R12 is suitable for low output pick-ups, but with higher output types there will be a large decrease in volume when the effect is switched in. To avoid this, R12 should be made around 22k in value if the unit is used with high output pick-ups. The current consumption of the unit is about 5 milliamps from the PP3 size 9 volt battery.

Construction

Details of the component panel and wiring a provided in Figures 2.15, 2.16, and 2.17. The stripboard panel has 50 holes by 19 copper strips. Some suppliers sell stripboard in 50 hole lengths, and the board can conveniently be a 19 strip wide piece cut from one of these standard size boards. Construction of the board is very straightforward, but as the components are packed in quite densely

Figure 2.15 The component layout of the stripboard panel. This has 50 holes by 19 strips

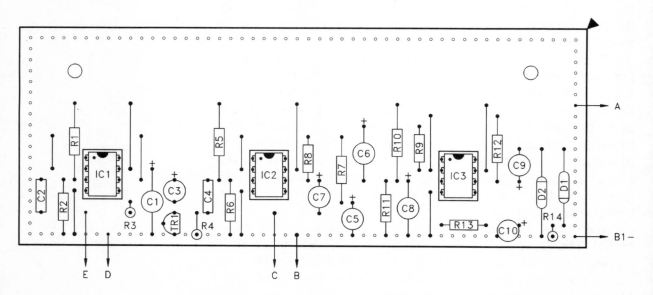

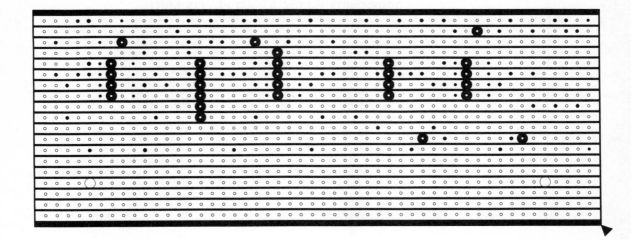

Figure 2.16 The underside of the stripboard panel

in places, take due care to avoid accidental short circuits between copper strips. TR1 is a form of MOS semiconductor, but it has a built-in zener protection diode. This makes anti-static handling precautions unnecessary.

S1 should be a heavy-duty push-button switch mounted on the top panel of the case, so that it can be operated by foot. Incidentally, most switches of this type are successive operation switches. In other words, activating them once switches the effect in, a second operation switches the effect out again, another operation switches it in again, and so on. This avoids having to keep your foot on the switch all the time the effect is required. On the other hand, switches of this type tend to be a bit slow in use, and can be rather noisy. An ordinary (non-latching) push-button switch is better if you require silent operation, or will need to switch the effect rapidly in and out. However, you may find it difficult to obtain a suitably tough switch of this type.

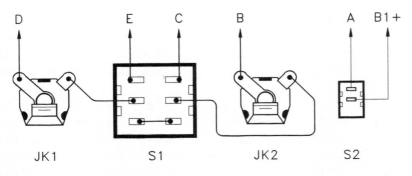

Figure 2.17 The compressor hard-wiring (use in conjunction with Fig 2.15)

45

Components (Compression effects unit)

Resistors
(all 0.25 watt 5% carbon film)

R1	100k	×4
R2	100k	—
R3	33k	×3
R4	100k	—
R5	470k	×2
R6	470k	—
R7	10k	×3 = 10·08
R8	100k	—
R9	10k	—
R10	33k	—
R11	33k	—
R12	220k (see text)	×1
R13	10k	—
R14	82k	×1

Capacitors

C1	100u 10V radial elect	0·10
C2	470n polyester	0·25
C3	1u 10V radial elect	0·10
C4	100n polyester	0·13
C5	2u2 10V radial elect	0·10
C6	2u2 10V radial elect	0·10
C7	10u 10V radial elect	0·10
C8	1u 10V radial elect	0·10
C9	4u7 10V radial elect	0·10
C10	4u7 10V radial elect	0·10

Semiconductors

IC1	LF351N	— 0·38
IC2	LF351N	— 0·38
IC3	LF351N	— 0·38
D1	1N4148	— 0·03
D2	1N4148	— 0·03
TR1	VN10KM or similar N	0·44
	channel VMOS transistor	

Miscellaneous

S1	d.p.d.t. heavy-duty push-button switch	2.51
S2	s.p.s.t. sub-min toggle	0·73
B1	9 volt PP3 size	
JK1	Standard jack socket	0·33
JK2	Standard jack socket	0·33
	Stripboard having 50 holes by 19 copper strips	
	Small plastic or metal case	
	8 pin d.i.l. i.c. holder (3 off)	0·00
	Battery connector	0·10
	Wire, solder, etc.	1·23

23·25

Auto-waa

The waa-waa effect is one that is probably familiar to all players of electric guitars. This effect is produced using a filter that boosts a narrow range of frequencies. This effect is usually in the form of a standard pedal type unit, where depressing the pedal raises the filter's frequency, and releasing it reduces its frequency. This type of unit can be rather awkward for the do-it-yourself enthusiast due to the difficulties in producing the pedal mechanism, which must control a potentiometer.

There are ways around this problem, and one of these is to have some form of automatic waa-waa effect. In this case the effect is a dynamic one, where the operating frequency of the filter is controlled by the volume of the signal being processed. The higher the level of the input signal, the higher the centre frequency of the bandpass filter. When applied to a guitar this gives a high initial filter frequency on each note, but the centre frequency quickly falls as the amplitude of the signal drops. This effectively gives a one way (high to low) sweep of the filter, giving what is more of a waa effect than a true waa-waa type. It is still quite an interesting and musically useful effect though.

If a conventional pedal controlled waa-waa effect is required, the circuit is easily modified to suit this method of operation. This is a subject that is explored in detail in the next section of this book.

Circuit operation

Figure 2.18 shows the full circuit diagram of the auto-waa unit. IC1 operates as a non-inverting amplifier having a voltage gain of about 28 times. For high output guitar pick-ups this level of voltage gain will be excessive, causing the signal to clip and distort at the output of IC1. To avoid this, R4 should be reduced to about 27k if the unit is used with high output pick-ups.

The bandpass filter is based on IC2, and it is has what is virtually a standard filter configuration. With this type of filter there are two capacitors (C6 and C7) and two resistors (R6 and R10) which control the operating frequency and other characteristics of the filter. In this case things are complicated by the inclusion of R5 and IC2. IC2 is a CMOS complementary pair and inverter, but here we are only using one of its N channel MOSFET transistors. This transistor can be used as a voltage controlled resistor, in just the same way as the VMOS transistor in the compression unit described previously. In effect, R2 and the resistance of IC2 shunt R6, and boost the operating frequency of the filter. The higher IC2's control voltage, the lower its resistance, and the higher the filter's operating frequency.

The control voltage for IC2 is generated by first slightly amplifying some of the output from IC1. This is the purpose of IC4 which operates as a non-inverting amplifier having a voltage gain of two

Figure 2.18 The auto-waa circuit diagram. IC2 acts as a voltage controlled resistor

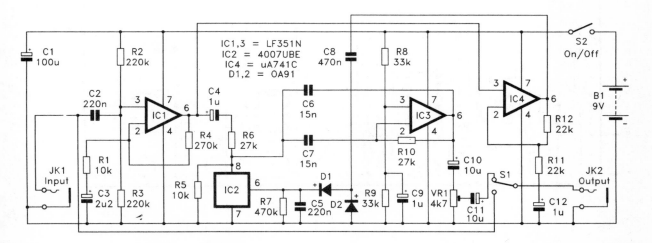

times. The output of IC4 is fed to a conventional rectifier and smoothing network based on D1 and D2. Germanium rather than silicon diodes are used here, as their lower voltage drop is an advantage in this application. Using silicon diodes the filter frequency would tend to drop back to its minimum level while the output from the guitar was still at quite a high level. The attack time of this circuit is very short, so that the filter frequency almost instantly jumps to a high frequency at the beginning of each note. The decay time is much longer, but is still short enough to ensure that the circuit accurately tracks the falling amplitude of each note.

S1 provides in/out switching by connecting output socket JK2 either direct to the guitar pick-ups, or to the output of the auto-waa unit. The output level of the circuit is likely to be greater than the output from the guitar, particularly if it is used with low output pick-ups. VR1 enables the output level to be reduced, and in practice VR1 is adjusted so that the subjective volume level is much the same whether the effect is switched in or out. The current consumption of the circuit is approximately 5 milliamps.

Construction

The stripboard component layout, stripboard underside, and hard wiring are illustrated in Figures 2.19, 2.20, and 2.21 respectively. There are a few important points to note when constructing this project. Firstly, IC2 is a CMOS device, and it therefore requires the standard anti-static handling precautions (see Chapter 1). Even if you do not bother with holders for the other integrated circuits, a holder

Figure 2.19 The auto-waa component layout. The board has 50 holes by 21 strips

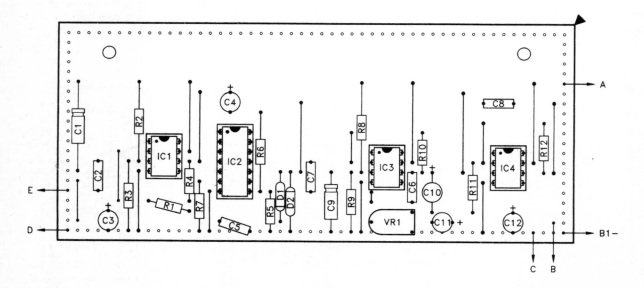

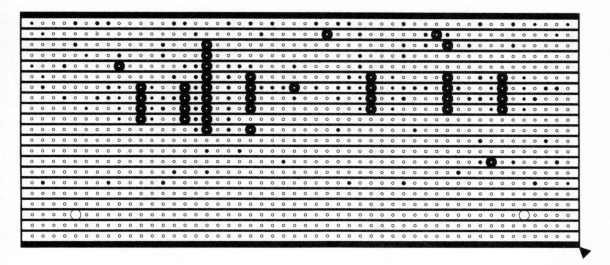

Figure 2.20 The underside of the auto-waa board

should certainly be used for IC2. Note that this device must be an unbuffered type having the UBE suffix, not a buffered device having just a BE suffix. Most component suppliers seem to stock only the unbuffered version, so there should be no problem here. D1 and D2 are germanium diodes, and as such are more vulnerable to heat damage than the more common silicon devices. Take due care when fitting these components to the board.

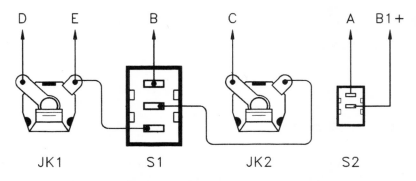

Figure 2.21 The auto-waa point-to-point wiring

Quite a good effect should be obtained using the specified component values, but the effect can be fine-tuned to your personal preference by altering the value of R12. If its value is made higher, the filter will tend to cover a higher range of frequencies. Making it lower in value will result in the filter never reaching the highest frequencies, even if the guitar is played very hard. With the specified value you should find that playing gently results in the filter never exceeding middle frequencies, while playing loudly takes the filter to the upper reaches of the audio range. This leaves plenty of scope for using the effect expressively, and is my preferred setup.

Components (Auto-waa)

Resistors		
(all 0.25 watt 5% carbon film)		
R1	10k	×2
R2	220k	×2
R3	220k	
R4	270k (see text)	×3
R5	10k	
R6	27k	
R7	470k	×1
R8	33k	×2
R9	33k	
R10	27k	
R11	22k	
R12	22k	×2

=10·08

Potentiometer	
VR1	4k7 min hor preset 0·15

Capacitors		
C1	100u 10V axial elect	0·10
C2	220n polyester	0·20
C3	2u2 10V radial elect	0·10
C4	1u 10V radial elect	0·10
C5	220n polyester	0·20
C6	15n polyester	0·17
C7	15n polyester	0·17
C8	470n polyester	0·25
C9	1u 10V radial elect	0·10
C10	10u 10V radial elect	0·10
C11	10u 10V radial elect	0·10
C12	1u 10V radial elect	0·10

Semiconductors		
IC1	LF351N	0·38
IC2	4007UBE	0·15
IC3	LF351N	0·38
IC4	uA741C	0·23
D1	OA91	0·15
D2	OA91	0·15

Miscellaneous		
S1	s.p.d.t. heavy-duty push-button switch	2·51
S2	s.p.s.t. sub-min toggle	0·23
B1	9 volt PP3 size	
JK1	Standard jack socket	0·33
JK2	Standard jack socket	0·33
	Stripboard having 50 holes by 21 copper strips	1·36
	Small plastic or metal case	3·70
	8 pin d.i.l. i.c. holder (3 off)	0·06
	14 pin d.i.l. holder	0·06
	Battery connector	0·10
	Wire, solder, etc.	1·23

£23·75

Waa-waa pedal

The auto-waa circuit is easily modified to work as a conventional waa-waa pedal. From the electronic point of view a waa-waa pedal is a much easier prospect. The voltage controlled resistor and its control circuitry can all be omitted and replaced with a potentiometer. Figure 2.22 shows the resultant waa-waa circuit. This operates in the same basic manner as the auto-waa unit, but with the filter frequency being controlled manually via VR1.

From the mechanical point of view things are much more difficult. Unless you have three hands, the potentiometer must be operated via a foot-pedal mechanism. In my experience of this type of thing, it is not too difficult to improvise a simple pedal mechanism, especially if you opt for one based on a slider potentiometer.

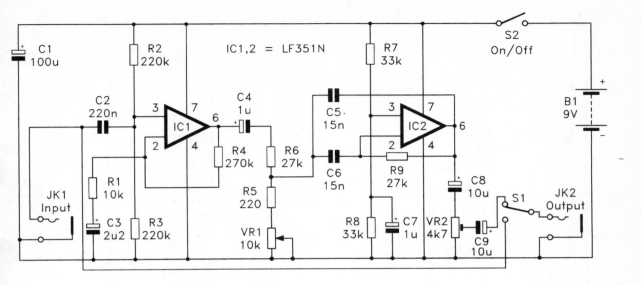

Figure 2.22 The waa-waa pedal
circuit diagram

However, producing something that will stand up to the rigours of everyday use is another matter. Improvised pedals seem to need constant attention to keep them in working order.

Unless you are good with things-mechanical, a more practical approach is to base the unit on an existing swell pedal. A conventional (non-electronic) swell pedal has a pedal mechanism which drives a potentiometer, but it may be necessary to change the potentiometer. The swell pedals I have used as the basis of home constructed effects units came complete with a 100k logarithmic potentiometer. This has to be changed for a 10k linear type in this case. Obviously any wiring to the potentiometer also has to be removed, together with any plugs, leads, etc. There should be sufficient space inside the swell pedal for the circuit board, battery, etc.

Clearly, before attempting to build this waa-waa pedal you need to be absolutely certain that by one means or another you can solve the difficulties associated with the pedal mechanism. If you are not sure that you have that side of things fully conquered, then it would be better to settle for the auto-waa unit instead.

Details of the stripboard component panel are shown in Figure 2.23 (top side) and Figure 2.24 (underside). The hard wiring is shown in Figure 2.25. The board has 36 holes by 21 copper strips. Electrically, construction of the unit is very straightforward and should present no difficulties. The current consumption of this manual version of the unit is only about 3 milliamps incidentally. Like the automatic version of the unit, R4 should be reduced to about 27k for operation with high output guitar pick-ups.

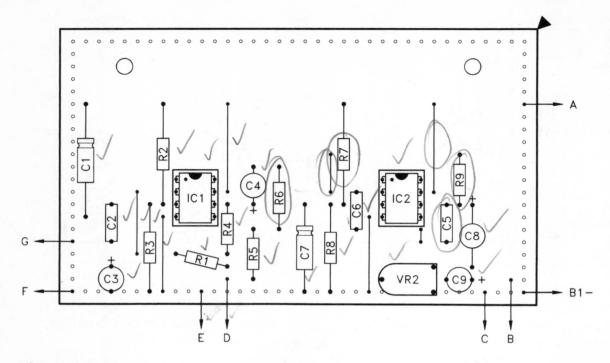

Figure 2.23 The waa-waa pedal component layout. The board has 36 holes by 21 strips

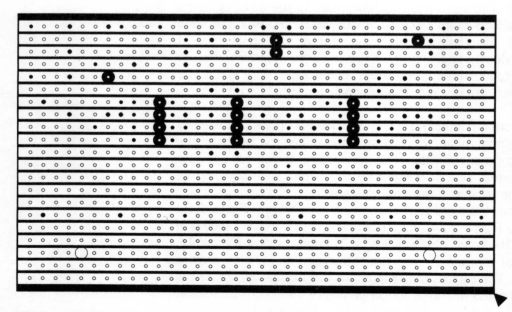

Figure 2.24 The underside of the waa-waa pedal board

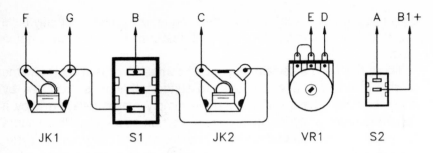

Figure 2.25 The waa-waa pedal hard wiring

Components (Waa-waa pedal)

Resistors
(All 0.25 watt 5% carbon film)
R1   10k
R2   220k
R3   220k
R4   270k (see text)
R5   220R
R6   27k   M27
R7   33k   M33
R8   33k
R9   27k   m27

Potentiometers
VR1   10k lin
VR2   4k7 min hor preset

Capacitors
C1   100u 10V axial elect
C2   220n polyester
C3   2u2 10V radial elect
C4   1u 10V radial elect
C5   15n polyester   0·15
C6   15n polyester
C7   1u 10V radial elect
C8   10u 10V radial elect
C9   10u 10V radial elect

Semiconductors
IC1   LF351N   LF351N
IC2   LF351N

Miscellaneous
S1   s.p.d.t. heavy-duty push-
       button switch
S2   s.p.s.t. sub-min toggle
B1   9 volt PP3 size
JK1   Standard jack socket
JK2   Standard jack socket
Stripboard having 36 holes
by 21 copper strips
Small plastic or metal case
Pedal mechanism (see text)
8 pin d.i.l. i.c. holder (2 off)
Battery connector
Wire, solder, etc.

Phaser

The phaser effect is a standard one which will no doubt be familiar to most readers. The basic effect is produced by sweeping a 'notch' of high attenuation up and down over the full audio frequency spectrum, or a large part of it anyway. It is a sort of inverse of the waa-waa effect, with its peaky response characteristic. A single notch does not produce a very strong effect, and most phasers actually have a two or three notch filter. The unit featured here is a twin notch type.

There has been a certain amount of confusion caused by the name of this effect, which would tend to suggest that it is produced by phase shifting. Phase shifting a signal simply means delaying it by a certain number of cycles, or a certain fraction of a cycle. Phase shifts are usually expressed in degrees, and there are 360 degrees per cycle. A phase shift of 180 degrees is therefore a shift of half a cycle, while one of 720 degrees is a shift of two cycles. Simply varying the phase of an audio frequency signal does not have a very noticeable effect on its sound. A large amount would give a sort of vibrato effect, but small amounts are not detectable by the human hearing mechanism.

A phaser does use phase shift circuits, but as a means of generating the notches in its frequency response. The phase shifting is not directly responsible for the phaser effect. The basic scheme of things is to have the phase shifted and unprocessed signals fed to a mixer. Signals that are in-phase will add together and emerge from the mixer increased in level. Signals that are out-of-phase will cancel out to some degree, and emerge from the mixer at a reduced level. If the two signals are exactly half a cycle out-of-phase, and of equal amplitude, they will precisely cancel out, giving a notch of infinite attenuation.

A twin notch phaser of this type has a phase shift network which provides between 0 and 720 degrees of shift, depending on the input frequency. At 180 degrees and 570 degrees (360 plus 180 degrees) precise anti-phase signals are produced, and the required notches are generated. The phase shift network is voltage controlled so that the frequencies at which the notches are produced can be swept using a low frequency oscillator (l.f.o.).

Circuit operation

Figure 2.26 shows the full circuit diagram for the phaser. This is not particularly original, and uses the standard method of generating the phaser effect. IC1 simply acts as a buffer stage at the input of the unit. This feeds into four identical phase shift circuits based on IC3 and IC5. Each section of the phase shift circuit provides between 0 and 180 degrees, giving the required 0 to 720 degrees total shift. In order to give the required voltage control of the phase shift circuit, one resistor in each section must be a voltage controlled type. The four voltage controlled resistances are provided by N channel MOSFETs in IC2 and IC4. This is much the same as the method utilised for the auto-waa circuit, but in this case two MOSFETs per 4007UBE are being used. IC6 is the mixer stage, and this is a conven-

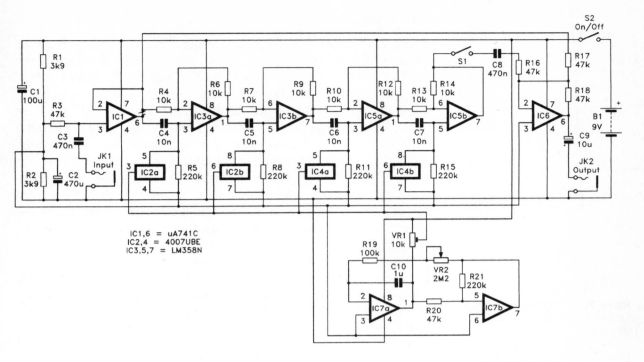

Figure 2.26 The twin notch phaser circuit diagram

tional summing mode type. S1 enables the phase shifted signal to be disconnected from the mixer, and the phaser effect to be switched out.

The low frequency oscillator uses IC7 in a standard triangular/ squarewave oscillator circuit. In this case it is the triangular signal from pin 1 of IC7 that is used, so that the phase shift network is swept smoothly up and down in frequency. The squarewave signal would simply switch the filtering between two pairs of notch frequencies, and would not give a worthwhile effect. VR1 is adjusted to give a suitable sweep range, and it is just a matter of setting this for what you subjectively regard as being the best effect. VR2 enables the sweep frequency to be adjusted from approximately 0.5Hz at maximum value, to 10Hz at minimum value. The phasing effect is sometimes used with very low sweep rates, but in a guitar context anything much slower than about 1Hz is unlikely to be of much practical value.

Although this project is rather more complex than most of the others featured in this book, the current consumption is still only about 6 milliamps. A PP3 size battery therefore suitable as the power source. The unit will work properly with high and low output guitar pick-ups without any need to alter component values to suit one type or the other. Distortion is lower with low output pick-ups, but the signal to noise ratio is better with high output types. Overall results should be quite good with either type.

Construction

Figure 2.27 shows the component layout, Figure 2.28 has details of the underside of the component panel and Figure 2.29 details of the point-to-point wiring. The board has 61 holes by 36 copper strips. Some suppliers sell stripboard in long 36 strip wide pieces, and this board can conveniently be one cut from such a board. You may have to buy quite a large board in order to obtain one that will furnish a 61 hole length, and there will be a substantial amount left-over. Looking on the bright side, this will provide sufficient stripboard for a few of the other projects in this book. Some suppliers sell a strip-board that measures 39 strips by 62 holes. Rather than try to trim one of these down to size, I would be inclined to simply ignore the column of holes down one edge of the board, and three copper strips along the top.

This project is rather more complex than those described previously, and a little more care needs to be exercised when building it. It is one that could not really be recommended for beginners. Remember that the 4007UBE used for IC2 and IC4 is a CMOS device, and that it requires the usual anti-static handling precautions.

Figure 2.27 The phaser component layout. The board has 61 holes by 36 strips

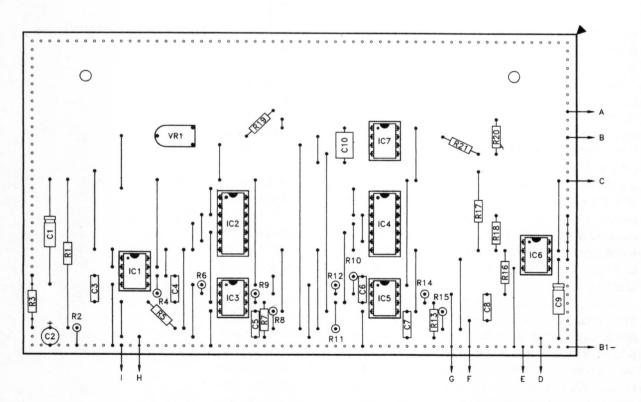

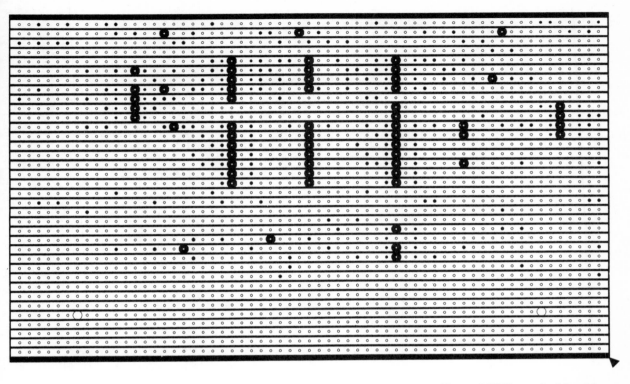

Figure 2.28 The underside of the phaser board

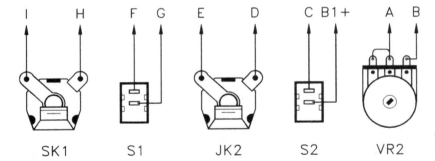

Figure 2.29 The phaser hard wiring (use in conjunction with Fig 2.27)

User tips

The phasing effect is one which works best with a signal that contains a wide range of frequencies. It is at its best with noise based sounds, and sounds which have a low pitch plus plenty of strong harmonics. In a guitar context it is best with a bass guitar plus a distortion unit (use the distortion unit ahead of the phaser). It is at its least effective with a straight guitar sound on high notes, where it will probably give a sort of tremolo effect.

Components

Resistors		
(all 0.25 watt 5% carbon film)		
R1	3k9	×2
R2	3k9	
R3	47k	×4
R4	10k	×8
R5	220k	×5
R6	10k	
R7	10k	
R8	220k	
R9	10k	
R10	10k	
R11	220k	
R12	10k	
R13	10k	
R14	10k	
R15	220k	
R16	47k	
R17	47k	
R18	47k	
R19	100k	×1
R20	47k	
R21	220k	

5×1·68

£8 40

Potentiometers
VR1 10k min hor preset   0·32
VR2 2M2 lin   0·15

Capacitors
C1 100u 10V axial elect   0·10
C2 470u 10V radial elect 0·23
C3 470n polyester   0·25

C4 10n polyester   0·11
C5 10n polyester   0·11
C6 10n polyester   0·11
C7 10n polyester   0·11
C8 470n polyester 8·25
C9 10u 10V axial elect 0·10
C10 1u polyester   0·38

Semiconductors
IC1 uA741C   0·23
IC2 4007UBE 0·15
IC3 LM358N   0·23
IC4 4007UBE 0·15
IC5 LM358N   0·23
IC6 uA741C   0·23
IC7 LM358N   0·23

Miscellaneous
S1 s.p.s.t. heavy-duty push-button switch   2·51
S2 s.p.s.t. sub-min toggle   0·73
B1 ~~9 volt PP3 size~~
JK1 Standard jack socket   0·33
JK2 Standard jack socket   0·33
Stripboard having 61 holes by 36 copper strips   1·66
Small plastic or metal case 3·2
8 pin d.i.l. i.c. holder (5 off) 0·0
14 pin d.i.l. i.c. holder (2 off) 0·
Control knob   0·20
Battery connector 0·10
Wire, solder, etc. 1·23

= £22·83

Dual tracking effects unit

The dual tracking effect, or 'mini chorus' as it also seems to be called, is a very simple effect in principle. You simply generate a delayed signal and mix it with the non-delayed signal. With one guitar plugged into the input, you effectively get a two guitar duet at the output. You can literally play a duet with yourself!

In reality this effect is not as easy to generate as one might hope. The problem is due to the more simple delay line methods not producing long enough delay times for this application. The delay time needs to be at least 10 milliseconds (one hundredth of a second) in order to give the required doubling up effect. With shorter delays the human ear does not perceive the output as being two separate sound

sources. The delay must be no more than about 60 milliseconds, as longer delays are perceived as a sort of short echo effect.

Although one hundredth of a second may not seem to be a very long time, it is practically an eternity in electronic terms. Simple delay lines give delays of millionths of a second rather than thousandths. These days the best way of obtaining fairly long delays in audio systems is to use a high resolution digital system. Unfortunately, this remains a complex and costly way of handling things. The only low cost alternative is an analogue delay line of the c.c.d. (charge coupled device) variety. These are popularly known as 'bucket brigade' devices, and are popular for use in a number of different types of musical effects unit.

A bucket brigade device basically consists of numerous electronic switches and capacitors. A capacitor can hold an electrical charge, which is analogous to a bucket holding water. In the bucket brigade analogy there is a line of buckets, and X amount of water is placed in the first one. This is then emptied into the second bucket, which is in turn emptied into the third one. Meanwhile, the first bucket is filled with Y amount of water. Its contents are emptied into bucket number two, and the contents of bucket number three is emptied into bucket number four. This basic process is continued, and eventually quantities X and Y will reach the end of the chain, and be discarded. In fact a continuous stream of water samples are taken at the input, and after a delay each one makes it along the chain to the output.

In the real delay line it is the input voltage that is sampled, and the sampled voltages are fed along the chain of charge storage capacitors until they reach the output. There is a slight problem at the output in that the last stage can not simultaneously provide an output signal and receive a sample from the previous stage. This means that the output voltage drops to zero while the last stage is receiving a sample. This gives a pulse signal which could be filtered to give an normal audio output signal, but it would require a massive amount of filtering. The more usual approach is to have an extra stage at the output, and to mix the signals from the last two stages of the delay line. This avoids the pulsing, but gives a stepped output signal. This is an inevitable consequence of a sampling system, and is caused by the signal jumping straight from one sample voltage to the next. However, relatively simple filtering is sufficient to smooth out this stepping and give a normal audio output signal.

A bucket brigade delay line needs to have at least several hundred stages in order to produce the delays required for chorus effects etc. Clearly this means using a complex circuit, but in practice reasonably simple circuits can be used as all the complexity is tucked away inside special c.c.d. delay line integrated circuits. This circuit is based on the MN3004 which has 512 delaying stages.

Circuit operation

Figure 2.30 shows the full circuit diagram for the dual tracking unit. IC3 is the delay line, and IC7 is the matching clock and bias generator chip. This produces a bias voltage needed by IC3, plus a two phase (anti-phase) clock signal. The clock signal controls the rate at which samples are passed through IC3.

In order to obtain good results the clock frequency must be at least double the highest input frequency, and should preferably be three or more times this frequency. In this case the clock frequency is just within the upper limit of the audio range at about 15kHz, which means that the audio bandwidth of the delay line must be limited to about 5kHz. This is obviously far less than the full audio bandwidth, but it is wide enough to give good results. Remember that this is the bandwidth of the delay line, and not that of the straight-through signal (which has the full 20kHz audio bandwidth). The delay time in milliseconds is equal to the number of delaying stages divided by double the clock frequency in kilohertz. This works out at around 17 milliseconds in this case, which is sufficient to give a good dual tracking effect.

The delay line chip is preceded by a lowpass filter based on IC2 which attenuates signals at excessive frequencies, and prevents them from producing significant amounts of aliasing distortion. IC1 is a buffer stage at the input of the unit. VR1 is adjusted to optimise the biasing of the circuit. IC4 acts as the mixer which combines the two output signals from IC3, and this is a conventional summing mode circuit. VR2 is adjusted to balance the two output signals so that there

Figure 2.30 The dual tracking unit circuit diagram. IC3 is the bucket brigade delay line chip

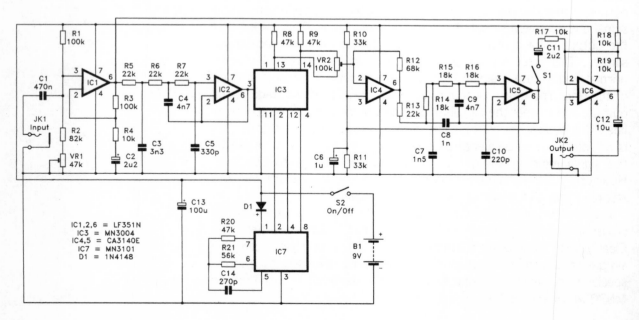

is minimal clock breakthrough at the output under quiescent conditions. IC5 is the buffer stage in a fourth order (24dB per octave) lowpass filter which removes the stepping on the output signal. IC6 is another summing mode mixer circuit, and this combines the delayed and non-delayed signals. S1 enables the delayed signal to be disconnected from the mixer, and this enables the effect to be switched in and out.

In order to obtain a low background noise level it is important that the delay line is driven with a high level signal of at least a few hundred millivolts r.m.s. The input buffer stage has been given a voltage gain of about ten times, so that the unit will give good results with low output guitar pick-ups. However, overloading will almost certainly occur if it is used with high output pick-ups. To avoid this, reduce R3 to about 10k in value if you will be driving the unit from high output pick-ups.

The circuit has a current consumption of about 14 to 15 milliamps. This is too high for a PP3 size battery, and I would recommend using six HP7 size cells in a plastic holder as the power source. The battery holder is fitted with a standard PP3 style connector incidentally.

Construction

The component side of the stripboard panel is shown in Figure 2.31, while Figures 2.32 and 2.33 respectively show the underside of the board and the hard wiring. The board has 64 holes by 26 copper strips. This is another project which is relatively complex, and which is not really suitable for a beginner. Even the more experienced constructors need to take due care when building this unit. Apart from the number of components and link wires that must be fitted to the board, construction of the unit is largely straightforward. Bear

Figure 2.31 The dual tracking unit component layout. IC3, IC4, IC5 and IC7 are all static sensitive devices

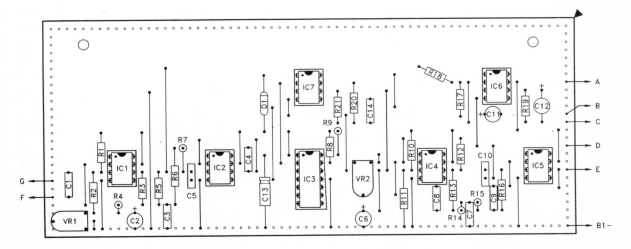

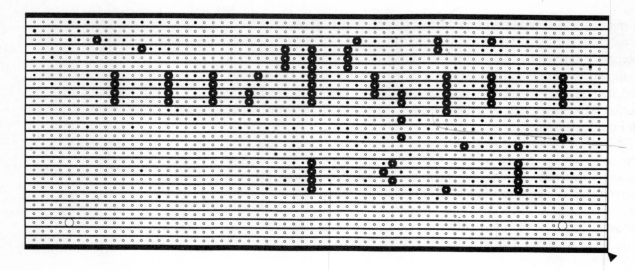

Figure 2.32 The underside of the dual tracking unit board. The stripboard panel has 64 holes by 26 copper strips

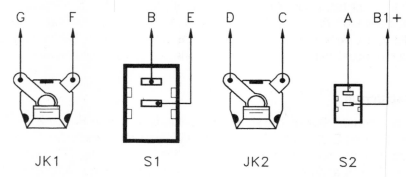

Figure 2.33 The dual tracking unit hard wiring

in mind though, that IC3, IC4, IC5, and IC7 are all MOS integrated circuits. Observe the standard anti-static handling precautions when dealing with these components.

Before connecting the unit into the system and switching on, make sure that both VR1 and VR2 are at roughly middle settings. Provided you have good hearing, you will be able to hear the slight clock breakthrough as a faint high-pitched whistle from the loudspeaker. By carefully adjusting VR2 it should be possible to null this signal, and render it totally inaudible. If the pitch of the clock breakthrough is too high for you to hear, temporarily add a capacitor of about 1n in value across C14 to reduce the clock frequency. This should give a clearly audible tone which can be minimised using VR2, after which the extra capacitor can be removed.

If suitable test gear is available (a sinewave or triangular waveform generator and an oscilloscope), VR1 is adjusted for symmetrical clipping using the standard techniques. If suitable test equipment is not available, simply give VR1 any setting that gives low distortion at high signal levels. Unlike VR2, its setting is not particularly critical.

Components (Dual tracking effects unit)

Resistors
(all 0.25 watt 5% carbon film)
R1 100k × 1
R2 82k × 1
R3 100k
R4 10k
R5 22k × 6
R6 22k
R7 22k
R8 47k × 3   9 × 1·68
R9 47k
R10 33k
R11 33k
R12 68k × 1   = 11·76
R13 22k
R14 18k × 3
R15 18k   6 × 1·68
R16 18k
R17 10k
R18 10k
R19 10k
R20 47k
R21 56k × 1

Potentiometers
VR1 47k min hor preset 0·15p
VR2 100k min hor preset 0·15

Capacitors
C1 470n polyester × 1 - 0·25
C2 2u2 10V radial elect × 2 - 0.20
C3 3n3 polyester × 1 - 0·11
C4 4n7 polyester × 2 - 0·22
C5 330p ceramic plate × 1 - 0·05
C6 1u 10V radial elect × 1 - 0·10

C7 1n5 polyester × 1 - 0·11
C8 1n polyester × 1 - 0·38
C9 4n7 polyester
C10 220p ceramic plate × 1 - 0·05
C11 2u2 10V radial elect
C12 10u 10V radial elect × 1 - 0·10
C13 100u 10V axial elect × 1 - 0·10
C14 270p ceramic plate × 1 - 0·05

Semiconductors
IC1 LF351N × 3 = 1·14
IC2 LF351N
IC3 MN3004 × 1 = 4·04
IC4 CA3140E × 2 = 0·80
IC5 CA3140E
IC6 LF351N
IC7 MN3101 × 1 = 1·15
D1 1N4148 × 1 = 0·03

Miscellaneous
JK1 Standard jack socket 0·33p
JK2 Standard jack socket 0·33p
S1 s.p.s.t. heavy duty push-button switch 2·51p
S2 s.p.s.t min toggle switch 0·73p
B1 9 volt (six HP7 cells in plastic holder)
Battery connector (PP3 type) 0·10
Stripboard having 64 holes by 26 copper strips 1·20
Medium-size plastic or metal box 3·27
8 pin d.i.l. i.c. holder (6 off) 0·04
14 pin d.i.l. i.c. holder 0·06
Wire, solder, etc. 1·23

100 × 100
= £34·70

Expander

The terms noise gate and expander seem to cause a certain amount of confusion, and they are definitely not simply different names for the same thing. However, they are designed to perform the same basic function, which is to give a boost in signal to noise ratio. These two types of device go about things in slightly different ways though.

A true noise gate a is form of electronic switch. It enables the input signal to pass through to the output only if the signal is above a certain threshold level. If the signal is below this level it is blocked, or possibly just attenuated by a substantial amount (typically 20dB or so). The reason for doing this is that the background noise is most

Photo 5 The expander board

noticeable when the signal level is very low, or is absent. At medium and high signal levels the noise tends to be masked by the main signal. By cutting off the signal when it is at a very low level an improvement in the signal to noise ratio is obtained. Perhaps it would be more true to say that there is an apparent improvement in the signal to noise ratio, since the noise level is as high as ever once the signal is switched through to the output.

An expander is a rather more sophisticated device, and its action is the opposite of the compressor unit described previously. As the input level rises, so does the gain of the circuit. In a noise reduction application the circuit would normally be arranged so that it has around 10dB to 12dB of attenuation at very low signal levels, reducing to no attenuation at high signal levels. Like a noise gate, it provides attenuation at low signal levels which reduces the background noise, and it therefore gives an apparent boost in the signal to noise ratio. At high signal levels there is no reduction in the noise, but the noise is masked by the main signal and will not be noticeable anyway.

Neither system is perfect, and the best one to choose depends on the prevailing circumstances. The main problem with a true noise gate in most situations is that it lacks subtlety. You do not need to have a particularly keen sense of hearing in order to detect the unit switching on and off. An expander is far less obvious provided the amount of expansion used is reasonably low, and it is introduced reasonably gradually. Obviously there is some distortion of the dynamic levels, but this will often not be apparent to the listener, and is often preferable to a high background noise level.

In a guitar context an expander is usually preferable to a noise gate, and the unit described here is a simple but versatile expander unit. It must be emphasised that an expander or noise gate can only combat noise on the input signal. If you have a noisy guitar amplifier there is no point in adding an expander ahead of it in an attempt to get a lower noise level. If a separate preamplifier is normally used ahead of the power amplifier, and this preamplifier is a bit noisy, then adding an expander between the preamplifier and the power amplifier would improve matters. With a guitar the problem is more likely to be in the form of hum pick-up, signals caused by unwanted acoustic pick up, or something of this type. An expander should be very effective at combatting this type of thing.

Circuit operation

The expander featured here can be used as a simple noise reduction unit, or it can be used as a simple effects unit. Compressing a guitar signal gives a better sustain – expanding it gives a more percussive and brief sound. This unit can built to have a small amount of expansion for noise reduction purposes, or a large amount in order to produce an interesting effect. Figure 2.34 shows the circuit diagram for the expander unit.

The circuit is based on a special compressor/expander integrated circuit, the NE570N (IC2). The NE571N is also suitable, as these two devices are virtually identical. The only difference is that the NE571N has slightly higher distortion figures, and is consequently a little cheaper. In this application the distortion performance of either device should be perfectly adequate – I used an NE570N merely because I had one of these in the spares box. These are dual expander/compressor devices, but in this application only one section is needed. No connections are made to the unused section.

Figure 2.34 The expander circuit diagram. Only one of the R6s should be used

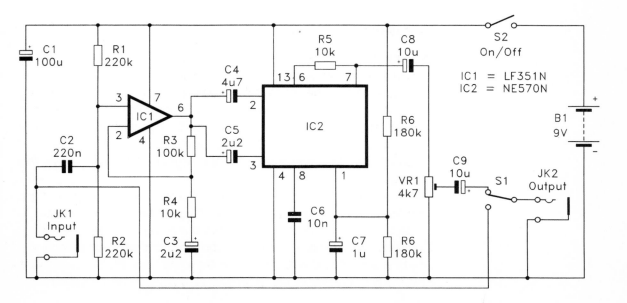

Each section of the NE570N consists of some electronic building blocks which can be configured as either an expander or a compressor. Obviously the expander setup is the one which is used here, and it is the more straightforward of the two. C4 and C5 couple the input signal to the gain control cell, and to the rectifier circuit which controls the gain cell. As the input level rises, so does the control voltage produced by the rectifier and smoothing circuit, and this causes the gain through the gain control cell to rise. This gives the required expansion effect. C7 is the capacitor in the smoothing circuit, and R5 is a feedback resistor in a buffer amplifier at the output of the circuit.

A simple distortion trimming circuit can be connected to pin 8, but unless you have some fairly advanced test equipment it is very difficult to get such a circuit set for optimum results. By simply using C6 here the circuit will achieve more than adequate distortion performance.

IC1 is used as an amplifier/buffer at the input of the unit. One purpose of IC1 is to provide the circuit with a suitably high input impedance. With a low output guitar pick-up it also provides a voltage gain of 20dB or so, which ensures that IC2 is driven at a high enough signal level. Note that with high output pick-ups IC1 will almost certainly be over-driven unless R3 is reduced to about 10k in value. At the output VR1 enables the signal level to be reduced to a level that is comparable to the direct output from the guitar pick-up. S1 provides in/out switching, and this simply switches JK2 between the direct output from the guitar and the output of the expander circuit.

Expansion characteristic

The standard expansion characteristic of the NE570N is a two to one type. In other words, a rise at the input of 10dB produces an increase at the output of 20dB, a 20dB increase at the input results in a 40dB increase at the output, and so on. This is quite a large amount of expansion, and is all right if you wish to utilise the circuit as an effects unit. It is too extreme for noise reduction purposes as the alterations to the guitar's dynamics are too obvious.

It is possible to alter the expansion characteristic by connecting a resistor from pin 1 of IC2 to the positive or negative supply rail. In the circuit diagram both these resistors are included (the two R6s). They have been given the same component number to emphasise the fact that you should only fit one or the other, not both. If you want to tame the expansion characteristic in order to use the circuit for noise reduction purposes, the upper R6 should be included. If you wish to make the expansion characteristic more extreme in order to give a stronger effect, include the lower R6.

The value of 180k is really only an example value, and it is worthwhile experimenting with values of around 120k to 1M in order to find the one that gives what you consider to be the best results. When experimenting like this it is a good idea to fit a couple of solder pins in the relevant pair of holes on the circuit board. It is then easy to fit and remove resistors of various values, with no risk of damaging the circuit board.

Construction

Details of the component layout are provided in Figure 2.35. The underside of the board and point-to-point wiring are illustrated in Figures 2.36 and 2.37 respectively. The board has 36 holes by 21 copper strips.

Bear in mind what was stated previously about R6. Do not include it at all for a straightforward two to one expansion characteristic, include the upper R6 to tame the characteristic for noise reduction purposes, or include the lower one to obtain a more extreme effect. IC2 is not a MOS device, but it is not a particularly cheap integrated circuit either. I would therefore strongly urge the use of a holder for this device.

Figure 2.35 The expander component layout. The board has 36 holes by 21 strips

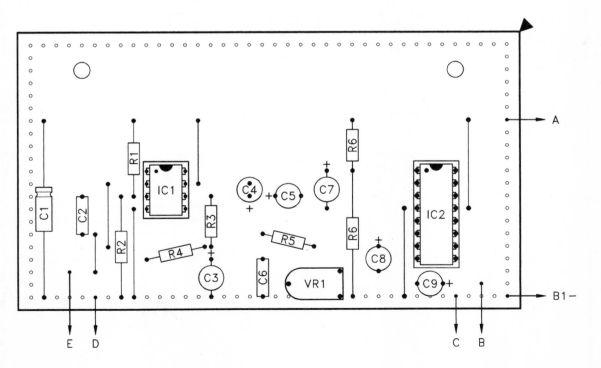

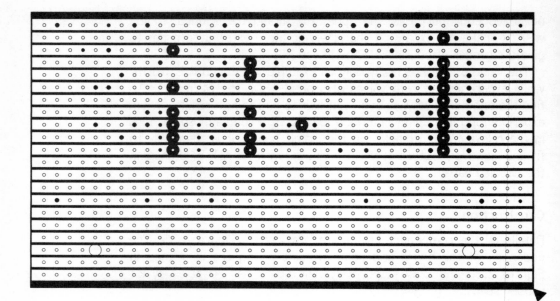

Figure 2.36 The underside of the expander board

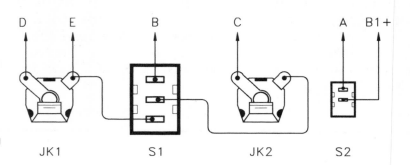

Figure 2.37 The point-to-point wiring of the expander

Components (Expander)

Resistors		Capacitors	
(all 0.25 watt 5% carbon film)		C1	100u 10V axial elect
R1	220k	C2	220n polyester
R2	220k	C3	2u2 10V radial elect
R3	100k (see text)	C4	4u7 10V radial elect
R4	10k	C5	2u2 10V radial elect
R5	10k	C6	10n polyester
R6	180k (see text)	C7	1u 10V radial elect
		C8	10u 10V radial elect
Potentiometer		C9	10u 10V radial elect
VR1	4k7 min hor preset		
		Semiconductors	
		IC1	LF351N
		IC2	NE570N or NE571N

Miscellaneous		B1	9 volt (PP3 size)
JK1	Standard jack socket		Battery connector
JK2	Standard jack socket		Stripboard having 36 holes
S1	s.p.d.t. heavy duty push-button switch		by 21 copper strips
			Small plastic or metal box
S2	s.p.s.t min toggle switch		8 pin d.i.l. i.c. holder
			16 pin d.i.l. i.c. holder
			Wire, solder, etc.

Treble booster

A treble booster must be the most simple of electronic guitar effects units. As the name suggests, it simply boosts treble frequencies, rather like turning up the treble using an ordinary tone control. However, the amount of boost is generally somewhat more than that provided by a treble tone control (a maximum of about 20dB or so, as opposed to the 12dB or thereabouts provided by most tone controls). This gives a much brighter sound, which is well suited to many types of music.

It is important that the treble boost should be introduced gradually, so that it is as inconspicuous as possible. It is especially important that the response should be free from any resonances. Another crucial factor is the frequency at which significant boost starts to be introduced. Making this frequency too high results in the unit having little effect. Making this frequency too low results in the fundamental frequencies sometimes being given a large amount of boost. This can cause overloading of the guitar amplifier.

Figure 2.38 shows the approximate frequency response of the prototype treble booster unit. Using a basic 6dB per octave boost characteristic (i.e. doubling the frequency gives a doubling of gain)

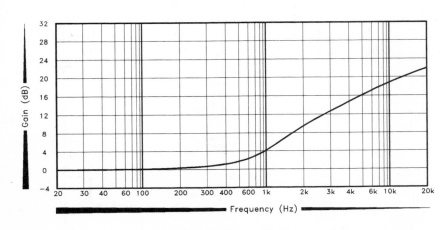

Figure 2.38 The approximate frequency response of the treble booster

ensures that the filtering is not too obvious, but still gives a worthwhile amount of boost. The maximum boost is about 22dB at 20kHz, and is a useful 12dB to 20dB over the important 3kHz to 10kHz range. The response is tamed, and rises very little above 20kHz. This helps to minimise problems with high frequency instability and radio frequency breakthrough. There is little boost at frequencies below about 1kHz or so, which ensures that the fundamental frequencies will normally receive little or no boost.

Circuit operation

As can be seem from the circuit diagram of Figure 2.39, the treble booster is basically just an operational amplifier used in the non-inverting mode. With S1 open the effect is switched out. IC1 operates as a unity voltage gain buffer stage with 100% negative feedback via R3. With S1 closed the effect is introduced, and the values of R3 and R4 give a voltage gain of eleven times. The value of C3 is much lower than would normally be used though, and at low to medium frequencies its impedance is very high. This impedance is in series with R4, and prevents R4 from significantly boosting the gain of the circuit. At higher frequencies the impedance of C3 becomes quite low in comparison to that of R4, and the gain is boosted. At about 20kHz or so saturation point is reached, and the full voltage gain of the circuit is achieved.

Figure 2.39 The treble booster circuit diagram

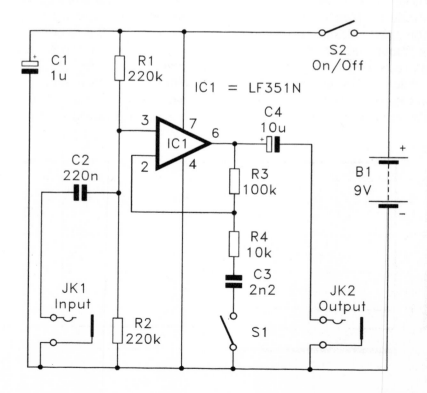

70

The current consumption of the circuit is only about one milliamp or so. A PP3 size battery is more than able to supply this.

Construction

Details of the component layout are shown in Figure 2.40, while Figure 2.41 shows the underside of the board. The point-to-point wiring is shown in Figure 2.42, which should be used in conjunction with Figure 2.40. The stripboard panel has 18 holes by 20 copper strips. Construction of the unit is extremely simple, and the unit is well suited to beginners to electronic project construction.

User tips

When using the unit remember that it introduces extra gain to the system, and that this will increase risk of problems with stray pickup and feedback. With high output pick-ups the extra gain at high frequencies is unlikely to cause any problems, but there is a greater risk when using low output pick-ups. Use a high quality cable to connect the guitar to the treble booster, and be careful to keep the guitar well away from the speakers. Obviously a unit of this type can only boost treble signals that are actually there to be boosted. Some guitars have a brighter output than others. In general, the pick-up nearest the bridge provides the most treble output, and results will be at their brightest if only this pick-up is selected.

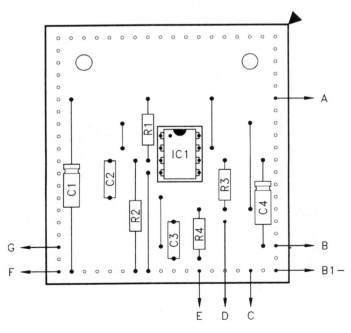

Figure 2.40 The component layout for the treble booster. The board has 18 holes by 20 copper strips

Figure 2.41 The underside of the treble booster board

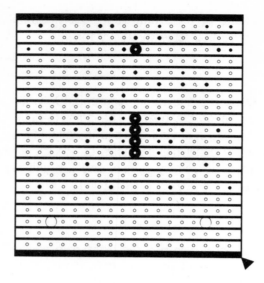

Figure 2.42 The treble booster wiring diagram

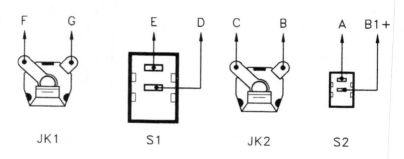

JK1   S1   JK2   S2

Components (Treble booster)

Resistors		Miscellaneous	
(all 0.25 watt 5% carbon film)		JK1	Standard jack socket
R1	220k	JK2	Standard jack socket
R2	220k	S1	s.p.s.t. heavy duty push-button switch
R3	100k		
R4	10k	S2	s.p.s.t min toggle switch
		B1	9 volt (PP3 size)
Capacitors			Battery connector
C1	1u 10V axial elect		Stripboard having 18 holes by 20 copper strips
C2	220n polyester		Small plastic or metal box
C3	2n2 polyester		8 pin d.i.l. i.c. holder
C4	10u 10V axial elect		Wire, solder, etc.
Semiconductor			
IC1	LF351N		

Dynamic treble booster

There is a slight problem with a simple treble booster in that the increased gain it provides inevitably results in a higher background hiss level. Although the gain is boosted only at high frequencies, and it is only the high frequency noise that is boosted, it is this high pitched hiss that tends to be the most noticeable. In fact some noise reduction systems operate by reducing the high frequency gain. Treble boost therefore acts as a very efficient noise booster. With a high output guitar pick-up the problem is likely to be minimal, since the voltage gain in the system will not be very high even at high frequencies. With low output pick-ups the gain in the system will be something like ten times higher, giving a correspondingly higher noise level.

Circuit operation

A simple way around the problem is to use a dynamic treble booster, which is a device that only applies the boost when the signal level is reasonably high. The signal from the guitar is then high enough to mask the background noise. Figure 2.43 shows the circuit diagram for a modified version of the treble booster which has this dynamic control of the boost.

The basic treble booster circuit is almost exactly the same as the original. However, instead of connecting direct to earth, S1 connects to earth via the drain to source resistance of an N channel MOSFET. The latter is one of the MOSFETs in a CMOS 4007UBE (IC3). If this

Figure 2.43 The circuit diagram for the dynamic treble booster

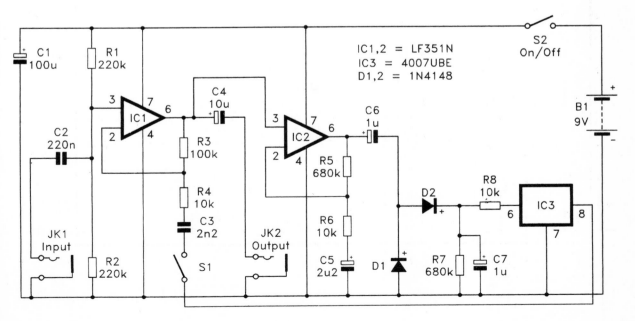

transistor is switched on (and S1 is closed), the treble boost will be introduced. If the MOSFET is switched off, the boost will not be applied regardless of S1's setting. The MOSFET will not necessarily be fully turned on or off, and will sometimes be in an intermediate state. An intermediate amount of treble boost will then be produced.

The control voltage for IC3 is generated by first amplifying some of the output signal using a non-inverting amplifier based on IC2. The output from IC2 is then rectified and smoothed to produce a positive d.c. control signal. Under standby and low input signal levels the output voltage from this circuit is too low to switch on IC3. At higher signal levels IC3 is brought into conduction, and the treble boost is produced.

R5's value effectively controls the threshold level at which the treble boost is introduced. Increasing its value gives a lower threshold – reducing its value gives a higher threshold level. The specified value should suit low output guitar pick-ups, but higher output types might require a lower value. It is probably worthwhile experimenting a little with the value of this resistor in order to find one that introduces the treble boost at the optimum threshold level for your particular setup.

Although the current consumption of this circuit is somewhat higher than that of the original treble booster design, it is still only about 3 milliamps or so. A PP3 size battery is therefore perfectly adequate to power this project.

Figure 2.44 The dynamic treble booster component layout. The board has 39 holes by 20 copper strips

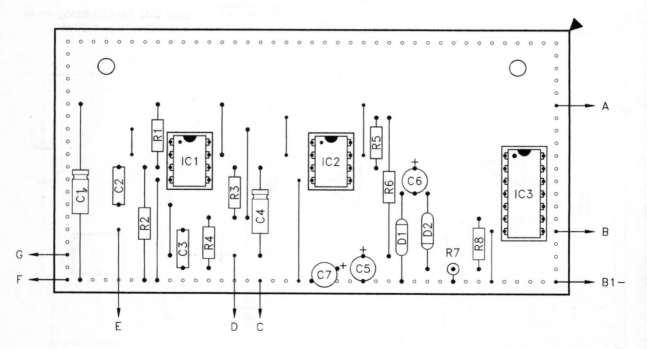

Construction

Details of the component layout can be found in Figure 2.44, while Figure 2.45 shows the underside of the component panel. Figure 2.46 shows the point-to-point wiring, and this diagram should be used in conjunction with Figure 2.44. The stripboard panel measure 39 holes by 20 copper strips.

Once again, construction is very straightforward and presents nothing out of the ordinary. Remember that IC3 is a CMOS integrated circuit, and that the standard anti-static handling precautions should therefore be observed when dealing with this device.

Figure 2.45 The underside of the dynamic treble booster board

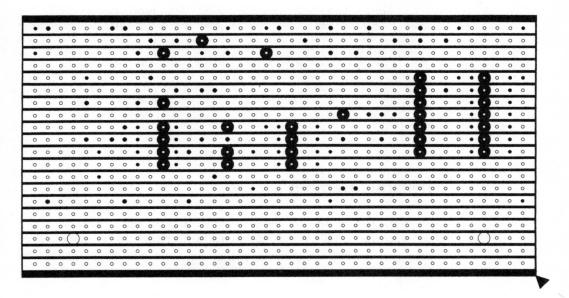

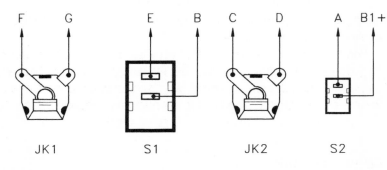

Figure 2.46 The dynamic treble booster hard wiring

Components (Dynamic treble booster)

Resistors		Semiconductor	
(all 0.25 watt 5% carbon film)		IC1	LF351N
R1	220k	IC2	LF351N
R2	220k	IC3	4007UBE
R3	100k	D1	1N4148
R4	10k	D2	1N4148
R5	680k		
R6	10k	Miscellaneous	
R7	680k	JK1	Standard jack socket
R8	10k	JK2	Standard jack socket
		S1	s.p.s.t. heavy duty push-button switch
Capacitors		S2	s.p.s.t min toggle switch
C1	1u 10V axial elect	B1	9 volt (PP3 size)
C2	220n polyester		Battery connector
C3	2n2 polyester		Stripboard having 39 holes
C4	10u 10V axial elect		by 20 copper strips
C5	2u2 10V radial elect		Small plastic or metal box
C6	1u 10V radial elect		8 pin d.i.l. i.c. holder (2 off)
C7	1u 10V radial elect		14 pin d.i.l. i.c. holder
			Wire, solder, etc.

Dynamic tremolo

Tremolo is one of the earliest of electronic music effects, and I suppose that in all honesty it has to be regarded as a rather out of date and boring. This unit breathes new life into an old effect by having the speed of the effect linked to the amplitude of the input signal. The higher the input level, the higher the speed of the effect. When applied to an electric guitar signal this means that the effect starts at a high rate of around ten or so cycles per second, and drops back to around one cycle per second as each note decays to a low level. This gives a much more interesting effect than using a fixed modulation frequency, which tends to be a bit monotonous when applied to such a simple effect.

For those who are not familiar with the tremolo effect and how it is produced, it should perhaps be explained that it is basically just amplitude modulation. In other words, the volume of the signal is varied by a control signal that is normally obtained from a low frequency oscillator. This gives a sort of throbbing sound.

Circuit operation

The circuit diagram for the dynamic tremolo unit appears in Figure 2.47. IC1 is a 4007UBE, and as in some of the previous projects, it

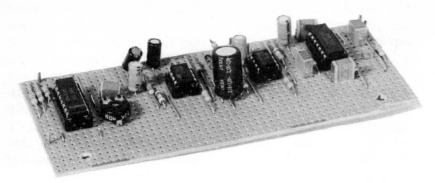

Photo 6 The dynamic tremolo board

is being used here as a voltage controlled resistor. Its resistance is connected as part of an attenuator network which has R1 as R2 as the other resistances. With zero control voltage to IC1 it has an extremely high resistance, and there are minimal losses through R1. As the control voltage to IC1 is increased, its resistance falls, and the losses through R1 increase.

R2 limits the maximum attenuation to 20dB or so, the exact figure depending on the output impedance of the guitar pick-up. This is sufficient depth for a good effect, and using greater depth will chop up the signal too much for most peoples' taste. However, you can reduce the value of R2 if you require more depth, or increase its value if you require a weaker effect. One of the advantages of do-it-yourself effects is that your can experiment with them, and set things up to suit your tastes rather than those of the designer.

IC2 acts as a buffer amplifier and it also provides a small amount of voltage gain to compensate for the losses through the voltage controlled attenuator circuit. S1 provides in/out switching, and it simply switches JK2 between the output of the tremolo circuit and the direct input from the guitar.

Figure 2.47 The dynamic tremolo circuit diagram. IC4 is a phase locked loop device but it is used here as a VCO

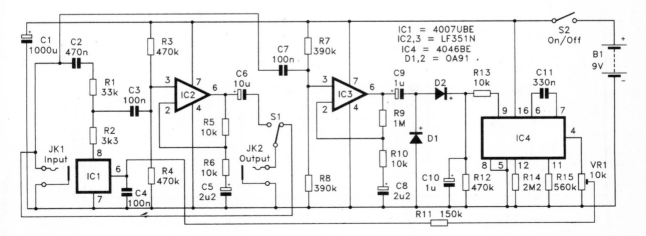

The low frequency oscillator is based on IC4, which is actually a low power phase locked loop device. In this circuit though, only its voltage controlled oscillator (v.c.o.) stage is utilised. The rest of the device is left unused, with no connections being made to the relevant pins. R15 and C11 are the oscillator timing components. The output from IC4 is a squarewave signal, which would simply switch the output signal between two levels. This would not give a very good effect, and a smoother transition from one signal level to the other is required. R1 and C4 form a simple lowpass filter which slows up the transition and gives a smoother effect. The output level of the v.c.o. is excessive, and so VR1 is used to attenuate this signal to a more suitable level.

A control signal for the v.c.o. is generated by first amplifying some of the input signal using IC3. The output of IC3 is then rectified and smoothed to produce a positive d.c. signal that is roughly proportional to the input signal level. In its original form there was a slight problem with the circuit in that the oscillator tended to cease oscillation before the input signal had decayed to an insignificant level. This is presumably due to the small voltage drops through the diodes producing an inadequate output voltage on low level input signals. To combat this problem R14 was added. This resistor simply keeps the oscillator operating even with zero control voltage, but at a low frequency of about 1Hz. This ensures that the tremolo effect is always present, and that it can not drop-out prematurely. If you would prefer a lower hold-on frequency, make R14 higher in value.

The specified value for R9 is suitable for low output guitar pick-ups. With high output types the tremolo effect will tend to linger too long at high modulation rates unless R9 is reduced to about 100k in value.

Figure 2.48 The component layout for the dynamic tremolo unit. The board has 51 holes by 20 copper strips

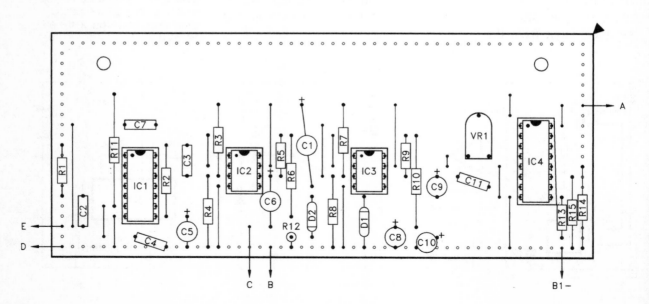

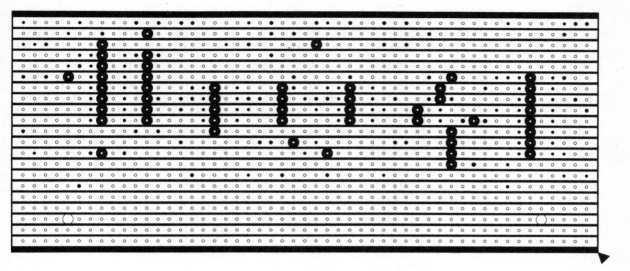

Figure 2.49 The underside of the dynamic tremolo board

The current consumption of the circuit is only about 3 to 4 milliamps. Like most of the other projects in this book, it can be powered from a PP3 size 9 volt battery.

Construction

Figure 2.48 and Figure 2.49 respectively show the component layout and underside of the stripboard panel. Figure 2.50 (in conjunction with Figure 2.48) shows the hard wiring. The stripboard panel has 51 holes by 21 copper strips. Bear in mind that both IC1 and IC4 are CMOS devices which require the standard anti-static handling precautions. Also, D1 and D2 are germanium diodes which are vulnerable to heat damage. Take due care not to damage D1 and D2 when soldering them into circuit.

When first testing the unit have VR1 set in a fully anti-clockwise direction. The unit should then pass the signal straight through to the output, providing a small boost in signal level. Gradually advancing VR1 should soon result in the tremolo effect being introduced. The

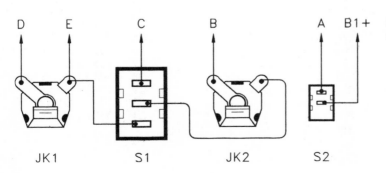

Figure 2.50 The dynamic tremolo unit hard wiring

correct setting for VR1 is with this component advanced just far enough to fully introduce the tremolo effect. This should give a good smooth modulation effect. Advancing VR1 too far will probably result in a rather abrupt and unpleasant modulation effect.

There is a potential problem with any effects unit that uses an oscillator in that there is a risk of switching 'clicks' from the oscillator finding their way into the signal path. The first prototype suffered from this affliction quite badly when it was used with a low output pick-up. The problem is less severe with high output pick-ups, because having an output level ten or so times higher results in any background noise being ten times or more lower in comparison to the guitar's signal.

The click problem with the original prototype was improved in two ways. Firstly, C1 was raised from 100u to 1000u. This effectively eliminated the coupling of the switching glitches from the oscillator to the audio circuitry via the supply lines. Secondly, the component layout was modified to give lower coupling through the stray capacitance between the copper strips on the component panel.

Provided the unit is built exactly to the design published here, and the wiring from the board to JK1 is either kept very short or a screened lead is used, switching clicks should be at a very low level. They might be apparent under no-signal conditions when using a low output guitar pick-up, but they should not be noticeable when the guitar is being played. It should be possible to reduce the click level still further by carefully removing pieces of copper strip that do not carry any interconnections. Another way is to use a preamplifier (such as the one described previously) ahead of the tremolo unit, so that it is handling a higher signal level.

Components (Dynamic tremolo)

Resistors
(all 0.25 watt 5% carbon film)

R1	33k
R2	3k3
R3	470k
R4	470k
R5	10k
R6	10k
R7	390k
R8	390k
R9	1M (see text)
R10	10k
R11	150k
R12	470k
R13	10k
R14	2M2
R15	560k

Potentiometer
VR1   10k min hor preset

Capacitors

C1	1000u 10V radial elect
C2	470n polyester
C3	100n polyester
C4	100n polyester
C5	2u2 10V radial elect
C6	10u 10V radial elect
C7	100n polyester
C8	2u2 10V radial elect
C9	1u 10V radial elect
C10	1u 10V radial elect
C11	330n polyester

continued

Semiconductors		S1	s.p.d.t. heavy duty push-button switch
IC1	4007UBE		
IC2	LF351N	S2	s.p.s.t min toggle switch
IC3	LF351N	B1	9 volt (PP3 size)
IC4	4046BE		Battery connector
D1	OA91		Stripboard having 51 holes
D2	OA91		by 21 copper strips
			Small plastic or metal box
Miscellaneous			8 pin d.i.l. i.c. holder (2 off)
JK1	Standard jack socket		14 pin d.i.l. i.c. holder
JK2	Standard jack socket		16 pin d.i.l. i.c. holder
			Wire, solder, etc.

Direct injection box

A direct injection (DI) box must be one of the most simple electronic devices you will find in today's hi-tech electronic music systems. This DI box has just seven components plus the batteries and on/off switch. As a DI box is not one of the best known pieces of equipment it would perhaps be as well to explain its purpose before proceeding further.

Many mixing and recording setups are designed for use only with high quality microphones, and accordingly have low level balanced line inputs. There are problems in using such an input with a signal source such as a synthesiser or a guitar. The easiest one to overcome is the relatively high output level of a guitar pick-up. A simple two-resistor attenuator is all that needed in order to bring a signal of a few hundred millivolts r.m.s. down to around one millivolt r.m.s. The balanced line problem is slightly more tricky, and requires some active circuitry.

Normally audio signals are carried by two signal lines; an earth wire and a non-earth or 'hot' wire, as some would term it. In a balanced line system there are still two signal wires, but neither are at earth potential. You have what are in effect two hot signal wires, and the audio signal is in the form of a voltage difference across these two wires. The point of using a balanced line system is that any stray pickup of hum and other noise should affect both lines equally. The stray pickup therefore generates no voltage difference between the two signal wires, and there is effectively zero pickup.

In practice it is not possible to rely totally on the balancing system to effectively eliminate any stray pickup. There will be imbalances in the system which will prevent perfect cancelling, and the amount of pick-up could be so large as to overload the input and cause severe noise problems. The balanced line system is normally used in conjunction with an earthed screen lead, effectively making it a three-wire system. There are still only two signal wires though, because the earthed screen lead is merely a screen, and is non-essential. The point of this belt and braces approach is that it produces insignificant levels of stray pick-up even if very long microphone cables are used in an electrically noisy environment.

Converting the output from a guitar to suit a balanced line system is quite simple, and it is basically just a matter of feeding the guitar's output to two buffer amplifiers. One must be an inverting type, while the other must be of the non-inverting variety. This gives anti-phase output signals which generate the required voltage differences across the two outputs.

Circuit operation

A DI box can be based on a couple of operational amplifiers, or a special dual balanced line driver integrated circuit can be used. The first method is the cheapest, but using a special line driver integrated circuit keeps things very simple and provides excellent performance. This DI box circuit (Figure 2.51) is based on the SSM2142 integrated circuit, which is a special balanced line driver type.

Unlike most of the projects in this book, two batteries are required for this project. These supply IC1 with dual balanced 9 volt supplies. C1 and C2 are supply decoupling capacitors which must be mounted very close to IC1 in order to prevent instability. Due to the use of

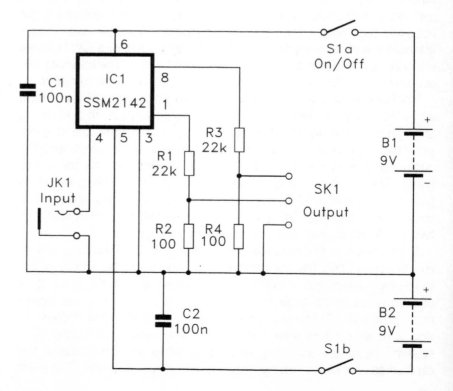

Figure 2.51 The direct injection box circuit diagram

dual balanced supplies there is no need for an input coupling capacitor, and the guitar is therefore direct coupled to the input of IC1.

On the output side of the circuit there are two attenuators, one on each output. A much better signal to noise ratio is obtained by having two attenuators at the output rather than one at the input. As the output of the unit will be feeding into a sensitive microphone input, it is advisable to use very low noise resistors in the attenuators, such as metal film types. With low output guitars results will probably benefit from having R1 and R3 reduced to about 2k2 in value, as the output level might otherwise be inadequate.

The current consumption is about 4 to 5 milliamps from each battery. PP3 size batteries will therefore have a reasonable long operating life. Note that a double pole on/off switch is needed for this project, one pole for each battery.

Construction

Figure 2.52 gives details of the component layout. Figure 2.53 shows the underside of the stripboard panel while Figure 2.54 shows the point-to-point wiring. The board has 17 holes by 19 copper strips. Construction of this project is so simple that it does not really require much comment. One point to note is that unlike the other projects in this book, this one does not use a jack socket at the output. A three way socket is required, and an XLR type is the normal choice for this type of thing. These are very high quality professional connectors which are quite expensive. A lower cost socket such as a three way DIN type could be used, but you would probably need to make up a DIN to XLR lead before you could use the DI box with anything.

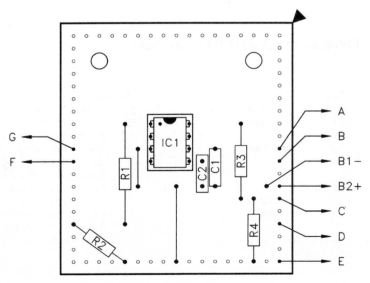

Figure 2.52 The DI box component layout. The board has 17 holes by 19 copper strips

Figure 2.53 The underside of the DI box board

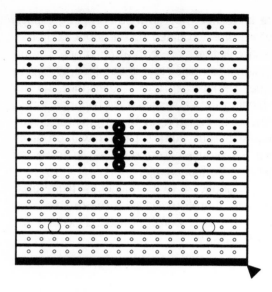

Figure 2.54 The DI box hard wiring. SK1 is an XLR connector

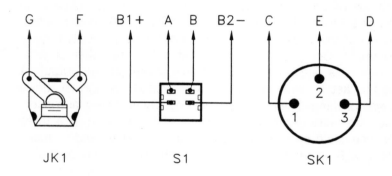

Components (Direct injection box)

Resistors
(all 0.25 watt metal film 1%)
R1   22k (see text)
R2   100R
R3   22k (see text)
R4   100R

Capacitors
C1   100n ceramic
C2   100n ceramic

Semiconductor
IC1   SSM2142

Miscellaneous
B1   9 volt (PP3 size)
B2   9 volt (PP3 size)
JK1   Standard jack socket
SK1   XLR connector (see text)
S1   d.p.s.t. miniature toggle switch
      Stripboard having 17 holes
      by 19 copper strips
      Small metal case
      Two battery connectors
      8 pin d.i.l. i.c. holder
      Wire, solder, etc.

Improved distortion unit

The distortion effects unit described earlier in this book gives quite a good effect, but not necessarily one that is to everyone's liking. In common with most distortion units, it provides a form of compression as well. This is due to the clipping method of generating the distortion. By clipping the signal at a certain level, it is obviously prevented from going above that level. The initial and middle parts of the signal are therefore all at this one level, giving a strong compression effect. In fact a soft clipping distortion unit does give some variation in output level during the initial stages of each note, but not very much. The degree of compression is still quite high even with soft clipping.

Another slight problem with simple distortion units is that it is difficult to control the distortion level. It is easy enough to vary the gain of the amplifier, and hence the degree of clipping, but in practice this does not seem to give quite the degree of control one would wish for. With hard clipping distortion units this method gives no real control at all.

Circuit operation

This 'improved' distortion unit provides a high degree of control over the distortion level, and it also largely retains the dynamic characteristics of the guitar's signal. It is not strictly speaking a better distortion effect, but a different distortion effect. Actually, a useful range of effects are possible. The circuit diagram for the improved distortion unit appears in Figure 2.55.

The circuitry around IC1 is much the same as that of the earlier unit. Like that circuit, it generates a soft distortion signal having a fair amount of compression. IC2 acts as a summing mode mixer which combines the direct input signal with the distortion signal from IC1.

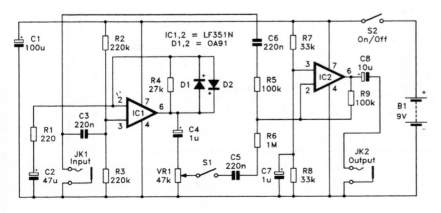

Figure 2.55 The circuit diagram for the improved distortion unit. This provides a mixture of distorted and unprocessed signals

VR1 permits the amount of distortion signal that is mixed with the direct signal to be accurately controlled. With VR1 set for minimum distortion, no distortion at all is added to the signal, and the normal characteristics of the guitar are retained. With VR1 set for maximum distortion, a thick distortion effect is obtained, with a fair amount of compression. The direct guitar signal is still present though, and the guitar's dynamic characteristics are still retained to a significant degree. Intermediate settings of VR1 permit in-between levels of distortion and sustain to be obtained. These intermediate settings provide some very good distortion effects.

S1 can be used to cut off the distortion signal from the mixer stage, and this provides a simple means of achieving in/out switching. The current consumption of the circuit is only about 3 milliamps, and a PP3 size battery is once again suitable as the power source.

The specified values for R1 and R6 are suitable for low output guitar pick-ups. If the unit will be used with a high output guitar, reduce R1 to about 2k2, and R6 to about 100k. This will ensure that IC1 produces a good quality soft distortion signal, and that the distortion and direct signal levels are reasonably well matched.

Construction

Figure 2.56 The improved distortion unit component layout. The board has 32 holes by 18 copper strips

Figure 2.56 shows the component layout of the stripboard panel. Figure 2.57 shows the underside view of the board. The stripboard panel has 32 holes by 18 copper strips. The point-to-point wiring is illustrated in Figure 2.58, which should be used in conjunction with Figure 2.57.

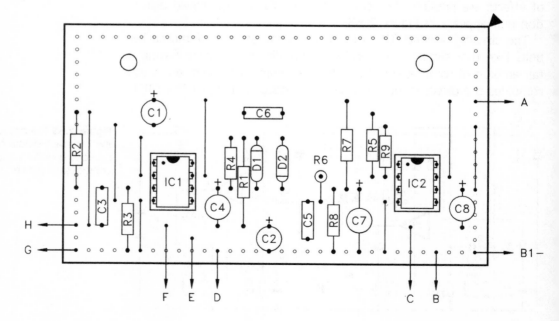

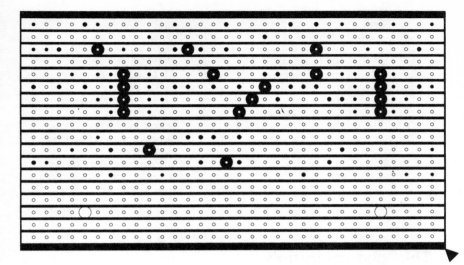

Figure 2.57 The underside of the improved distortion unit board

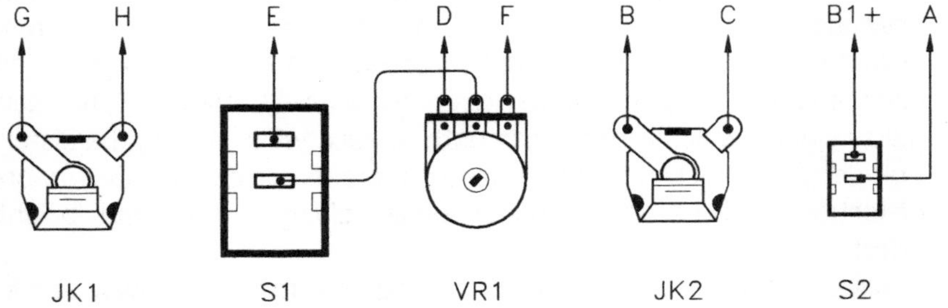

G H E D F B C B1+ A

JK1   S1   VR1   JK2   S2

Figure 2.58 The improved distortion unit hard wiring

This is another fairly simple project which should be quite easy to construct. Bear in mind though, that D1 and D2 are germanium diodes, so take care not to overheat them when soldering them onto the board. When using the unit, bear in mind that it is adding extra gain into the signal path, and that extra care will be needed in order to avoid problems with hum, feedback, etc.

Components (Improved distortion unit)

Resistors
(all 0.25 watt 5% carbon film)
R1   220R (see text)
R2   220k
R3   220k
R4   27k
R5   100k
R6   1M (see text)
R7   33k
R8   33k
R9   100k

Potentiometer
VR1   47k log

Capacitors
C1   100u 10V radial elect
C2   47u 10V radial elect
C3   220n polyester
C4   1u 10V radial elect
C5   220n polyester

continued

C6	220n polyester	Miscellaneous	
C7	1u 10V radial elect	JK1	Standard jack socket
C8	10u 10V radial elect	JK2	Standard jack socket
		S1	s.p.s.t. heavy duty push-button switch
Semiconductors			
IC1	LF351N	S2	s.p.s.t min toggle switch
IC2	LF351N	B1	9 volt (PP3 size)
D1	OA91		Battery connector
D2	OA91		Stripboard having 32 holes by 18 copper strips
			Small plastic or metal box
			8 pin d.i.l. i.c. holder (2 off)
			Wire, solder, etc.

Thin distortion unit

This device is another variation on the soft distortion project described previously. It basically differs from the improved distortion unit only in that the distortion signal is out-of-phase with the direct signal. This gives a cancelling effect which tends to severely attenuate the main guitar signal (which is present in both signals) while leaving the distortion largely intact. In other words there is proportionately more distortion and less normal guitar signal, giving a 'thin' and 'bright' effect.

Also, as the level of the distortion signal remains relatively stable, but the level of the direct signal varies significantly during the course of each note, the degree of cancelling varies during each note. A conventional distortion effect, in contrast to the direct output from the guitar, gives a sound that is largely free from variation during each note. This form of distortion unit therefore helps to give a more lively sound, more in keeping with the nature of the instrument.

Circuit operation

The full circuit diagram for the thin distortion unit appears in Figure 2.59. The circuitry around IC2 and IC3 is much the same as the soft distortion unit circuit. The only major difference is that IC2 is used in the inverting mode instead of the non-inverting type. This gives the required anti-phase relationship between the direct and distorted signals. It also results in the input impedance of the clipping amplifier being quite low at just 220 ohms. A buffer amplifier based on IC1 is therefore used to boost the input impedance of the circuit to a more suitable level of about 50k.

The current consumption of the circuit is about 4 milliamps from the PP3 size 9 volt battery. The specified value for R3 is suitable for

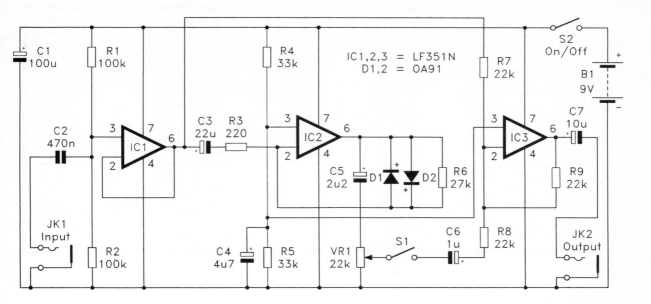

low output guitar pick-ups. For operation with high output types R3 should be increased to about 2k2 in value.

Figure 2.59 The thin distortion unit circuit diagram. It uses anti-phase mixing to attenuate the main guitar signal

Construction

Figure 2.60 shows the component layout of the stripboard panel, and Figure 2.61 shows the underside view. The hard wiring is illustrated in Figure 2.62 (which should be used in conjunction with Figure

Figure 2.60 The thin distortion unit component layout. The board has 44 holes by 20 copper strips

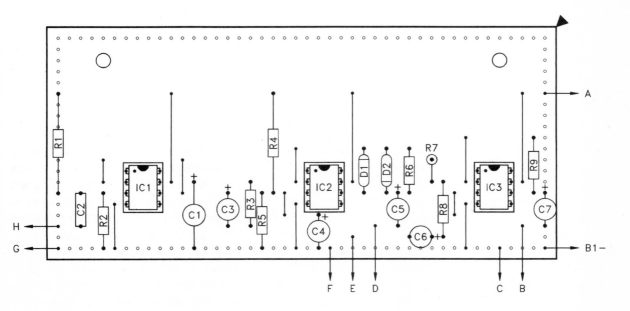

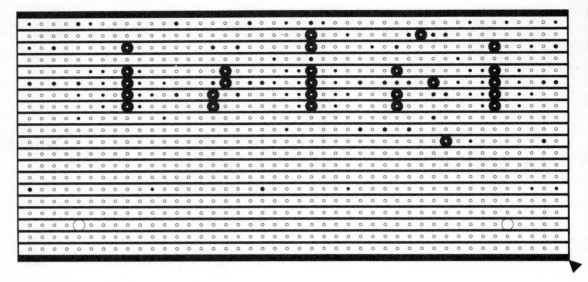

Figure 2.61 The underside of the thin distortion unit board

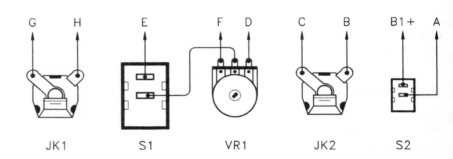

Figure 2.62 The thin distortion unit hard wiring

2.60). The board has 44 holes by 20 copper strips. Building the unit presents few difficulties, but remember that D1 and D2 are germanium devices, and take due care not to overheat these components when soldering them in place.

User tip

When using this unit, bear in mind that it is another project which adds gain in the signal path. Be more diligent about avoiding problems with stray pickup and feedback. With VR1 fully backed-off there will be no distortion added. Advancing it slightly will produce a small amount of distortion plus severe cancelling of the main signal when it has decayed to a low level. This gives quite a subtle but good distortion effect, where a largely undistorted signal decays into almost pure distortion. Stronger effects can be obtained by advancing VR1 further. It is worthwhile experimenting a little with the setting of this control to discover the variations in the effect that are available.

Components (Thin distortion unit)

Resistors
(all 0.25 watt 5% carbon film)
R1   100k
R2   100k
R3   220 (see text)
R4   33k
R5   33k
R6   27k
R7   22k
R8   22k
R9   22k

Potentiometer
VR1   22k log

Capacitors
C1   100u 10V radial elect
C2   470n polyester
C3   22u 10V radial elect
C4   4u7 10V radial elect
C5   2u2 10V radial elect
C6   1u 10V radial elect
C7   10u 10V radial elect

Semiconductors
IC1   LF351N
IC2   LF351N
IC3   LF351N
D1   OA91
D2   OA91

Miscellaneous
JK1   Standard jack socket
JK2   Standard jack socket
S1   s.p.s.t. heavy duty push-
       button switch
S2   s.p.s.t min toggle switch
B1   9 volt (PP3 size)
       Battery connector
       Stripboard having 44 holes
       by 20 copper strips
       Small plastic or metal box
       8 pin d.i.l. i.c. holder (3 off)
       Wire, solder, etc.

Guitar tuner

This project is a relatively simple tuning aid which will help you to quickly and easily get your guitar properly tuned. Traditional tuning methods are actually quite quick and easy, but only if you have a very good sense of pitch. It tends to be assumed that everyone who is musically talented has perfect pitch, but this is not the case. You can actually be a very competent musician without having a very keen sense of pitch. With this guitar tuning aid it is possible to accurately tune a guitar even if you are completely tone-deaf!

The main tuning indicator is a flashing l.e.d. This flashes at a rate which is equal to the difference between the frequencies of a reference tone and the guitar. Using the unit is therefore just a matter of selecting the right reference tone, plucking the appropriate string, and adjusting the string for a very low flash rate from the l.e.d.

There is an earphone output for a crystal earpiece, and this can be used to monitor the audio beat note produced by the interaction of the two tones. This is useful when initially setting up the unit. It is also very helpful when the guitar's tuning has been allowed to slip well out of tune, or a new string has been fitted. The l.e.d. may then flash at such a high rate that it will appear to light up continuously. The beat note will be audible from the earphone though, and this enables the guitar to be easily tuned to a point where the l.e.d. flashes perceptibly. The l.e.d. can then be used as the indicator for fine tuning the guitar string.

Circuit operation

Figure 2.63 shows the full circuit diagram of the guitar tuner. IC1 operates as a preamplifier which boosts the guitar signal to a level that can reliably drive the next stage. The voltage gain of IC1 is quite high at about 60dB (1000 times), which ensures that the unit will work even when the signal from the guitar has decayed somewhat. The gain will probably be excessive for high output pick-ups though, and for operation with these it would be advisable to reduce R3 to about 47k. C3 severely rolls-off the high frequency response of the preamplifier. This reduces noise and high frequency harmonics on the guitar signal, giving a cleaner signal into the subsequent stage of the circuit.

This next stage is a trigger circuit based on IC2. This simply produces a (more or less) square wave output signal at the fundamental pitch of the guitar signal. IC4 is a 555 astable (oscillator) circuit which has six switched timing resistors (VR1 to VR6). These preset resistors are adjusted for the correct reference tones. In other words, they are adjusted to give the same six frequencies as the six open strings on a correctly tuned guitar. A low power 555 is used for IC4 in order to keep the power consumption of the circuit down to a reasonable level.

IC3 is a quad 2 input NOR gate package, but in this case only one of the four gates is needed. The inputs of the other three gates are tied to one or other of the supply rails so that they are not left

Figure 2.63 The guitar tuner circuit diagram. Only one gate of IC3 is used

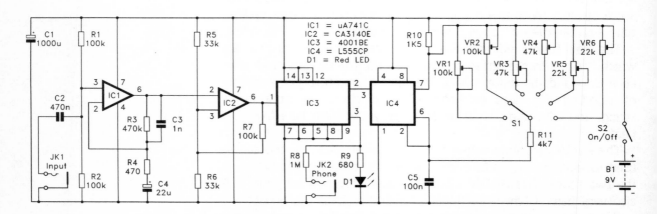

vulnerable to static charges, or spurious operations which would unnecessarily increase the current consumption of the circuit. The purpose of IC3 is to compare the outputs of the trigger circuit and the reference oscillator, and to produce the beat note at the difference in their frequencies. It drives l.e.d. indicator D1 via current limiting resistor R9, and the earphone socket by way of R8. The latter reduces the volume from the earphone to a less ear-aching level. Note that the output from this circuit will only drive a crystal earphone, and is totally unsuitable for any other type of headphone or earpiece.

There is a potential problem with a unit of this type, in that there is a definite tendency for modulations of the supply voltage to cause the reference oscillator to lock-on to the same frequency as the input signal when the two are at similar frequencies. This is clearly undesirable as it would limit the accuracy of the unit. To avoid this problem, supply decoupling capacitor C1 has been given a very high value of 1000u.

It is important that the reference oscillator provides stable frequencies that do not vary as the battery voltage drops due to aging. There is no need to bother with using a stabilised supply since the output frequency of a 555 oscillator is almost totally independent of the supply potential. The average current consumption of the circuit is about 10 to 16 milliamps, depending on the l.e.d. activity. I would therefore recommend using a fairly high capacity battery, such as six HP7 size cells in a plastic holder.

Construction

The component layout and underside of the stripboard panel are shown in Figures 2.64 and 2.65 respectively. The board has 49 holes by 23 copper strips. The hard wiring is illustrated in Figure 2.66.

While construction of this project is largely straightforward, there are a few points worth noting. IC2 has a PMOS input stage, and IC3 is a CMOS logic device. Consequently, both of these components require the standard anti-static handling precautions.

JK2 is a 3.5 millimetre jack socket, and not the standard 1/4in (6.35mm) type used in previous projects and for JK1. A 3.5 millimetre jack socket is the appropriate type to use simply because the crystal earphone will almost certainly be supplied fitted with a 3.5 millimetre jack plug. If you use a different type of socket it will be necessary to fit the earphone with a different plug, or to use the appropriate adaptor. The 3.5 millimetre jack sockets offered by most component retailers are of the open construction variety, and they have a switch contact. This switch is used to turn off the loudspeaker automatically when the earphone is in use. It is of no value in the

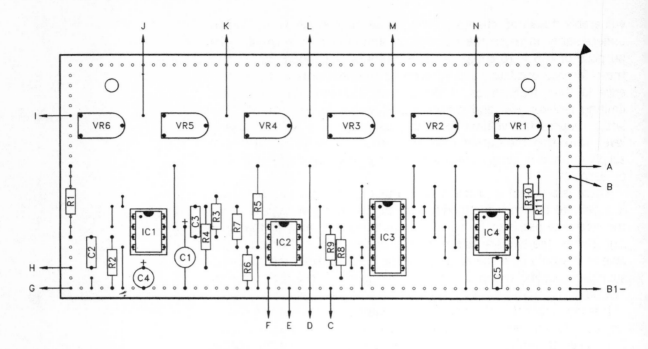

Figure 2.64 The guitar tuner component layout. The board has 49 holes by 23 copper strips

Figure 2.65 The underside of the guitar tuner board

present context, and accordingly it is left unused. Hence there are three tags shown on SK2 in Figure 2.66, but connections are made to only two of them.

In a similar vein, S1 is a standard 6 way 2 pole rotary switch. In this case we only need one pole of this switch. Consequently, no connections are made to one section of this switch, leaving seven tags unconnected. Most switches of this type have the pole terminals

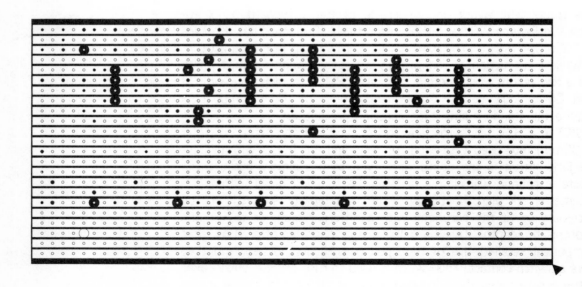

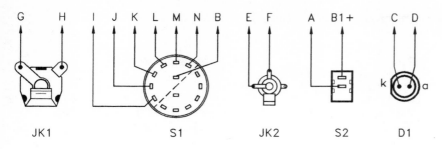

Figure 2.66 The guitar tuner point-to-point wiring

marked A and B, and the wiper contacts marked 1 to 12, making it easy to use the right terminals. In this instance it is the ones marked A and 1 to 6 that should be used.

The cathode (k) terminal of a l.e.d. is normally indicated by that lead being slightly shorter, and by a flat on that side of the case. This flattening of the case is not always very obvious, but it is usually there if you look carefully. Not all l.e.d.s actually have one or other of these methods of polarity indication, but you can as a last resort determine the correct polarity by trial and error. Connecting D1 around the wrong way will not damage it. You can use an ordinary l.e.d. for D1 plus a simple plastic clip to fit it to the front panel of the case, but in my experience this does not work well. The l.e.d.s rarely seem to clip securely into these simple holders. A l.e.d. plus a proper screw fixing holder, or a l.e.d. supplied complete with a screw fixing holder, is a much better choice, and well worth the small extra cost.

Setting up

Before the unit can be used you must give VR1 to VR6 suitable settings. In order to do this a correctly tuned electric guitar must be connected to the guitar tuner. Select VR1 and play the lowest string of the guitar. Adjust VR1 for a low flash rate from D1, using the beat note from the earphone to help you zero in on it. Then fine tune VR1 for the lowest flash rate you can achieve. There is a slight problem in that the unit will operate even if the reference tone and guitar are on different octaves. The l.e.d. flashes more clearly if the two tones are on the same octave though. It is therefore worth trying VR1 over virtually its full range of settings to find the one at which D1 provides the clearest indication. Once VR1 has been set up correctly, use the same basic method with the other strings of the guitar to set up VR2 to VR6. The unit is then ready for use.

Components (Guitar tuner)

Resistors
(all 0.25 watt 5% carbon film)
R1   100k
R2   100k
R3   470k (see text)
R4   470R
R5   33k
R6   33k
R7   100k
R8   1M
R9   680R
R10   1k5
R11   4k7

Potentiometers
(All min hor presets)
VR1   100k
VR2   100k
VR3   47k
VR4   47k
VR5   22k
VR6   22k

Capacitors
C1   1000u 10V radial elect
C2   470n polyester
C3   1n polyester
C4   22u 10V radial elect
C5   100n polyester

Semiconductors
IC1   uA741C
IC2   CA3140E
IC3   4001BE
IC4   L555CP or ICM7555CP
D1   Red panel l.e.d.

Miscellaneous
JK1   Standard jack socket
JK2   3.5mm jack socket
S1   6 way 2 pole rotary switch
S2   s.p.s.t min toggle switch
B1   9 volt (6 x HP7 size cells in
        holder)
        PP3 type battery connector
        Stripboard having 49 holes
        by 23 copper strips
        Small plastic or metal box
        8 pin d.i.l. i.c. holder (3 off)
        14 pin d.i.l. i.c. holder
        Wire, solder, etc.

Glossary

Amplitude modulation

This is where one signal varies the strength (amplitude) of another signal. In an electronic music/electric guitar context, a low frequency oscillator rhythmically varies the volume of the instrument to give the familiar tremolo effect.

Attenuate

If an electrical signal is made smaller, it is attenuated (e.g. if you back-off a volume control you are increasing the attenuation it provides.

Axial

Components which are tubular in shape and have a leadout wire coming from each end are axial types. Virtually all resistors and many capacitors are of this type.

Balanced line input

An input which has two terminals, neither of which are earths. This type of input combats unwanted pickup of electrical noise using a cancelling process. Screening is normally used as well, so as to give an extremely low level of stray pickup. This type of input is much used on professional mixing desks and other professional audio equipment. A direct injection (DI) box is needed in order to use a normal non-balanced signal source (which includes most guitars) with a balanced line input.

Bandpass filter

This is a circuit which only allows signals over a small range of frequencies to pass through to the output. Signals at other frequencies are greatly attenuated. Bandpass filtering is used to provide waa-waa effects.

Base

The name given to one of the terminals of a transistor.

Bifet

A term applied to integrated circuits which use a combination of ordinary (bipolar) and field effect transistors. Most devices of this type are operational amplifiers which are primarily intended for use in audio circuits. Devices of this type provide low noise and distortion levels.

Bucket brigade device

A popular name for delay lines which work by passing electrical charges along a chain of capacitors. They are more correctly termed charge coupled devices (c.c.d.s).

Capacitor

A common electronic component that can store an electrical charge. Normal capacitors can be connected either way round, but electrolytics and certain other polarised types must be connected with the correct polarity.

Carbon film

A type of resistor, and what is these days the 'standard' type.

Ceramic plate capacitor

These are miniature low value capacitors which are often only about 3 millimetres square and under a millimetre thick. They are not the highest quality components in some respects, but are adequate for most purposes.

Charge coupled device (c.c.d.)

See 'bucket brigade device'.

Chip

Modern semiconductors (transistors, integrated circuits, etc.) are basically chips of silicon. Any semiconductor component made from a silicon chip could be called a 'chip', but it is a term that is normally applied only to integrated circuits.

Clipping

This is where the peaks of a signal are chopped off, producing severe distortion. This occurs accidentally when an amplifier is over-driven, or deliberately to produce distortion, overdrive, and 'fuzz' effects (which are all terms for the same thing). Hard clipping simply chops off the signal peaks, while soft clipping gives a sort of rounding of the peaks. In terms of the sound produced, hard clipping gives much harsher distortion.

Clock

A clock oscillator (often just called a 'clock') is used in many electronic circuits to control the rate at which the circuit operates. For example, in a c.c.d. delay line the clock rate determines the rate at which samples are passed through the device, and it therefore controls the delay time.

CMOS

An acronym for 'complementary metal oxide silicon', a technology used in the production of some integrated circuits. These devices usually have very low current consumptions, and are static sensitive.

Collector

The name given to one of the terminals of a transistor.

Delay line

A circuit which delays the signal passing through it by a certain length of time. Delay lines are used a great deal in electronic music and with electric guitars as several popular effects are based on them (echo, flanging, chorus, etc.).

Diode

A simple electronic component which permits an electric current to flow in one direction, but not in the other. Diodes are semiconductors (like transistors and integrated circuits).

Direct injection (DI) box

See 'balanced line input'.

Disc ceramic

A type of capacitor, and one which is rather low in quality in some respects. However, disc ceramics have some qualities which make them ideal for certain applications.

Drain

The name given to one of the terminals of a field effect transistor (f.e.t.).

Dry joint

A soldered connection which does not provide a good electrical connection. A joint of this type will often be globular in appearance, possibly with a dull finish to the solder and a lot of burnt flux over and around the joint.

Dual in-line (d.i.l.)

Any component which has two identical rows of pins, side-by-side, is a dual in-line type. In practice it is mainly integrated circuits that have this type of pin arrangement, although it is used for a few other types of component.

E24 series

Resistors and capacitors are available only in certain values, popularly known as the E24 series (there being 24 values in each decade). Each value is very roughly 10% higher than the previous value. Some components are only available in every other value (the E12 series) or every fourth value (the E6 series).

Electrolytic

A type of capacitor. High value capacitors are mostly of the electrolytic variety. These are polarised capacitors which must be fitted the right way round if they are to function correctly.

Emitter

The name given to one of the terminals of a transistor.

Farad

Capacitance is measured in farads. A farad is a very large unit, and so most large capacitors have their value in marked in microfarads (millionths of a farad). Smaller capacitors have their values marked in nanofarads or picofarads. A nanofarad is one thousandth of a microfarad, and a picofarad is one thousandth of a nanofarad (or one millionth of a microfarad).

Field effect transistor (f.e.t.)

A type of transistor. F.e.t.s are used in some of the designs in this book as voltage controlled resistors. F.e.t.s and ordinary bipolar transistors have very different characteristics, and are definitely not interchangeable.

Flux

Solder for electrical and electronic use contains multiples cores of flux which help the solder to flow properly over the joint. This produces a good strong joint and a reliable electrical contact.

Frequency

Essentially another word for pitch. Frequency is expressed in hertz, and one hertz is one pressure wave, string vibration, or whatever, per second. Higher audio frequencies are measured in kilohertz (1000 hertz equals 1 kilohertz). The audio range is generally accepted as extending from 20 hertz to 20 kilohertz, although few people can actually hear the extremes of this range. The concert pitch middle A is at a frequency of 440 hertz.

Gain

Just another word for amplification.

Gate (1)

The name given to one of the terminals of a field effect transistor (f.e.t.).

Gate (2)

The most simple forms of logic integrated circuit (as used in computing, digital control systems, etc.). There are several different types of gate (NOT, AND, OR, NAND, NOR, XOR and XNOR).

Germanium

The substance from which the original transistors were made. These days most semiconductor components are based on silicon, but germanium is still used to some extent (mainly for diodes). Devices based on germanium are more vulnerable to heat damage than are silicon based components.

Hard clipping

See 'clipping'.

Hertz

See 'frequency'.

Integrated circuit (i.c.)

A semiconductor component which can provide the equivalent of anything from two to over a million components. Integrated circuits are much used in modern circuits as they permit quite complex circuits to be built at low cost.

Jack

A type of audio connector, much used for headphones and electronic music systems. Most guitars are fitted with standard (6.35mm/ 0.25 inch) jack sockets, as are all the projects in this book. There are also smaller (2.5mm and 3.5mm) types, and stereo versions, so you need to be careful to order the right type.

Kilohertz

See 'frequency'.

Kilohm

See 'ohm'.

Light emitting diode (LED)

A diode that produces light if it is fed with an electric current. Unlike an ordinary filament bulb, this is a polarised component which must be connected around the right way or it will not produce any light.

Linear (Lin)

See 'logarithmic'.

Logarithmic (log)

In an electronic project context this describes a type of potentiometer. It is one which has a form of non-linear control characteristic (e.g. it does not provide half maximum resistance when adjusted to a middle setting). This type of potentiometer is used in volume controls and similar applications, but linear potentiometers are used in virtually all other applications.

Megohm

See 'ohm'.

Metal film

A type of resistor, and a very high quality type.

MOS

An acronym for 'metal oxide silicon', and a form of technology used for producing some transistors and integrated circuits. Most MOS devices are sensitive to static electricity, and must be kept away from or protected from even modest static charges.

Multi-core

The type of solder used for electrical and electronic work (which includes electronic project building). The multiple cores in question are cores of flux.

Nanofarad

See 'farad'.

Notch filter

A filter that enables most signals to pass through to the output. However, signals over a small range of frequencies are greatly reduced, and may even be totally removed. Notch filtering is used to produce the phasing effect.

Ohm

The main unit of electrical resistance. One ohm is quite a small amount of resistance, and so resistances are often expressed in kilohms or megohms. One kilohm is one thousand ohms, and a megohm is one million ohms (one thousand kilohms).

Operational amplifier (op amp)

A general purpose amplifier that was originally designed for use in analogue computers (to perform mathematical operations). These days an operational amplifier is normally a small integrated circuit which is much used in audio and electronic music applications.

Oscillator

This is simply a circuit that generates a series of electrical pulses. Oscillators are much used in practically all types of electronic circuit.

Phase shift

This is where a signal is effectively delayed by a certain number of cycles, or a certain part of a cycle. Phase shifts are normally expressed in degrees, and there are 360 degrees per cycle. Thus a signal that is shifted by 180 degrees is delayed by half a cycle, and one which is shifted by 720 degrees is delayed by two cycles. Note that a phase shift and a true delay (as provided by a delay line) are not the same. The delay time provided by a phase shift circuit is frequency dependent. The higher the input frequency, the shorter the delay represent by 'X' number of cycles. A delay line provides a delay time that is independent of the input frequency.

Picofarad

See 'farad'.

Pin

This can either be a terminal of an integrated circuit (or other components with pin-like terminals), or a solder pin. Solder pins are connected to a circuit board, and then the connections from the board to off-board components are made via these pins. Solder pins are more convenient than direct connections to the board, and provide much more reliable results. One millimetre diameter pins are needed for the 0.1 inch stripboard used for the projects in this book.

Polarised

Normally used to describe a two lead component that must be fitted round the right way if it is to function properly (e.g. electrolytic capacitor). It is also used to describe plugs and sockets that have some sort of mechanical 'key' so that they can only be connected one way round.

Potentiometer

A variable resistor which has three terminals. Two terminals connect to opposite ends of the track which provides the resistance. There is a fixed resistance between these two terminals. The third connects to the 'wiper', and there is a variable amount of resistance between this and the other two terminals. This is the type of component used in volume controls, tone controls, etc.

Preset resistor

This is a form of potentiometer, or variable resistor. It is designed to fit onto a circuit board rather on a front panel. Preset resistors normally have to be adjusted using a small screwdriver, although some have a small built-in control knob.

Printed circuit board (PCB)

A printed circuit is a board on which electronic circuits are constructed. Stripboard is a form of proprietary printed circuit which can accommodate practically any circuit. Normal printed circuit boards are designed to take one particular circuit, and are unusable with any other circuits

Printed circuit (PC) mounting

A term which is used to describe components that have both leadout wires coming from the same end, and which are intended for vertical mounting on a printed circuit board. It is most often applied to capacitors, and these are also known as radial capacitors. Any component which is designed for direct mounting on a printed circuit board can be described as a PC type.

Radial

See 'printed circuit (PC) mounting'.

Rectifier

Much the same as a diode, but designed to handle much higher power levels.

Resistor

Common electronic component having two leadout wires. It can be connected either way round. The value is normally marked using a four band colour code (see page 5).

Ribbon cable

Simply a ribbon-like multi-way electrical cable. The 'rainbow' ribbon cable that has a different coloured insulation for each wire is very good for wiring-up electronic projects.

Semiconductor

Components such as diodes, transistors and integrated circuits which are made from a semiconductor material such as germanium or silicon.

Silicon

The substance from which most modern semiconductor components (transistors, diodes, integrated circuits, etc.) are constructed. Other substances are also used, such as germanium, but are relatively rare.

Soft clipping

See 'clipping'.

Solder pin

See 'pin'.

Source

The name given to one of the terminals of a field effect transistor (f.e.t.).

Stand-off

These are usually in the form of small plastic clips which are used to mount a circuit board inside a case, and hold the board a few millimetres clear of the case. Some types are fixed to the board and (or) the case via self-tapping screws, and these provide what is usually a much more reliable method of mounting.

Stray pickup

The wiring in an electronic project can act a bit like an aerial, and will pick up radio signals, 'hum' from mains wiring, etc. In an audio frequency project, which includes guitar effects units, this can result in unwanted 'buzzes' and other sounds on the output signal. Ideally, projects which have wiring that is vulnerable to this problem should be fitted in a metal case earthed to the circuit's negative supply rail. However, if all the wiring is kept very short there will usually be no significant pick-up if a non-metallic case is used. Audio leads should be good quality screened types in order to prevent then from picking up electrical noise.

Stripboard

A thin board made from an insulating material and drilled all over with 1mm diameter holes on a 0.1 inch (2.54mm) matrix (see Photo 4, page 19). Copper strips run along the rows of holes on one side of the board. All the projects in this book are based on a piece of stripboard.

Tinning

Tinning simply means covering something with a thin layer of solder. The end of a soldering iron's bit should be kept well tinned so that it makes good thermal contact with the joints. It is also a good idea to tin the ends of leads and tags prior to soldering them together.

Toggle switch

A switch that is operated via a small lever (called a 'dolly').

Transistor

A three terminal electronic component which can provide amplification. The terminals are called the base, collector and emitter.

Variable resistor

See 'potentiometer'.

Veroboard

A proprietary name for the stripboard which is used as the basis of all the projects in this book.

VMOS

A type of field effect transistor.

XLR

This is a heavy-duty form of three way audio connector which is used a great deal in professional audio equipment. In particular, it is used for balanced line inputs on professional mixing and recording equipment.

Index

Aliasing distortion, 60
Amplifier (headphone), 34
Amplitude modulation, 76
Analogue delay line, 59
Attack time, 44
Auto-waa effect, 46
Axial, 10

Balanced line input, 81
Bandpass filter, 46
Base, 12
Battery, 18
Battery clip, 18
Bifet, 31
Bit (soldering iron), 20
Boxes, 25
Break before make, 18
Bucket brigade device, 59
Buying components, 1

C.C.D., 59
Capacitor, 2, 7
Carbon film, 3
Cases, 25
Centre frequency, 46
Ceramic plate (capacitor), 8
Clipping, 37
Clock breakthrough, 61
Clock frequency, 60
CMOS, 14
Collector, 12
Colour code (resistor), 4,7
Components, 1
Compression effect, 42
Compressor, 42
Copper strips, 20, 28
Crystal earphone, 91
Cutting (copper strips), 20

D.P.D.T., 17
D.P.S.T., 17
Decay time, 44
Delay line, 60
Delay times, 58
DI box, 81
Diode, 2, 11

Direct injection (DI) box, 81
Disc ceramic (capacitor), 9
Distortion effect, 37
Distortion unit (improved), 85
Distortion unit (thin), 88
Dolly, 17
Drain, 13
Dry joint, 21, 28
Dual in-line (d.i.l.), 14
Dual tracking effect, 58
Dynamic treble booster, 73
Dynamic tremolo, 76

E24 series, 3
Electrolytic capacitor, 9
Emitter, 12
Expander, 63
Expansion characteristic, 66

Fault finding, 27
Faulty components, 27
Faulty construction, 28
Feedback problems, 90
Flux, 20

Gate, 13
Germanium diodes, 12
Getting started, 1
Guitar preamplifier, 30
Guitar tuner, 91

Handling precautions, 15
Hard clipping, 37
Hard wiring, 23
Headphone amplifier, 34
HP7 cells, 18

Improved distortion unit, 85
Insulated sockets, 17
Integrated circuit (i.c.), 2, 13
Integrated circuit holders, 15
Integrated circuit orientation, 15
Intermodulation distortion, 39

Jack connectors, 16

Kilohm, 3

Layout, 26

Light emitting diode (LED), 2
Linear (lin), 7
Link wires, 22
Logarithmic (log), 7
Low frequency oscillator, 78

Mail order, 2
Make before break, 18
Megohm, 3
Metal film, 3
Microfarad, 8
Mini chorus effect, 58
Modulation frequency, 76
MOS, 14
MOSFET, 47,54
Mounting bolts, 25
Mounting component boards, 25
Multi-cored solder, 22

N channel, 47
Nanofarad, 8
Noise reduction, 67
Noise gate, 63
NOR gate, 92
Non-inverting amplifier, 43
Notch filter, 53

Off-board components, 24
Ohm, 3
Oscilloscope, 62
Out-of-phase, 54
Over-heating, 12

PC capacitor, 10
Pedal effect (waa-waa), 50
Pedal mechanism, 51
Phase locked loop, 78
Phase shift, 54
Phase shift circuit, 54
Phaser, 53
Phasing effect, 53
Picofarad, 8
Pin numbering (i.c.), 16
Pins, 24
PMOS, 93
Polarised, 10
Polyester (capacitor), 8
Potentiometer, 6

Power amplifier, 34
Power rating, 4
PP3 battery, 18
PP9 battery, 18
Preamplifier, 30
Preferred values, 3
Preset resistor, 2, 7
Push-button switch, 18

Radial, 10
Rainbow ribbon cable, 23
Rectifier, 11
Reference oscillator, 93
Reference tone, 91
Resistor, 2, 3
Ribbon cable, 23
Rocker switch, 17
Rotary switch, 17

S.P.D.T., 17
S.P.S.T., 17
Sampling, 59
Screened lead, 81
Signal to noise ratio, 64
Sinewave, 37
Soft clipping, 38
Soft distortion, 37
Solder, 22
Solder bridges, 28
Solder pins, 24
Soldering, 20
Soldering iron, 22
Source, 13
Spacers, 25
Spaghetti wiring, 23
Stand-offs, 26
Standard jacks, 16
Static sensitive, 14
Step-by-step building, 27
Stereo headphones, 37
Stray pickup, 90
Stripboard, 19
Sustain effect, 42
Switches, 17

Testing, 27
Thin distortion, 88
Threshold level, 74
Tinning, 21, 24
Toggle switch, 17
Tolerance, 4,8
Transistor, 2, 12
Treble booster, 69
Treble booster (dynamic), 73
Tremolo (dynamic), 76

Trigger circuit, 92
Tuner (guitar), 91
Tuning aid, 91
Type numbers, 14

Veroboard, 19
VMOS transistor, 13
Voltage controlled attenuator (v.c.a.),
    77
Voltage controlled oscillator (v.c.o.), 78
Voltage controlled resistor, 77

Voltage gain, 31

Waa-waa pedal, 50
Watt, 4
Waveform generator, 62
Wire clippers, 20
Wire strippers, 24
Wiring-up, 23

XLR, 17, 83

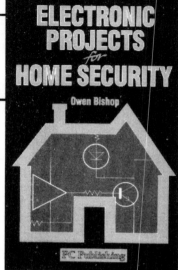

For newcomers to electronics

Digital Electronics
Projects for Beginners

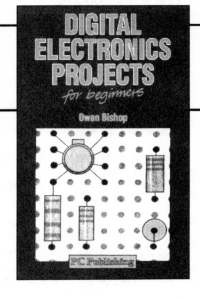

Owen Bishop

125pp · ISBN 1 870775 08 2
£6.95 (inc P&P)

✳ For newcomers to electronic
 construction
✳ Simple self build projects
✳ Gives full constructional details
✳ Serious practical uses

This book contains 12 digital electronics projects suitable for the beginner to build with the minimum of equipment. They cover a wide range of topics, from instrumentation to home security, and a few 'fun' projects as well. With one exception, all the projects are battery-powered, so are completely safe for the beginner.

The introductory chapter and the detailed explanations of the working of each project make this not only a book of practical projects but an introduction to the theory and applications of digital electronics.

Each project has a circuit diagram, a drawing of the stripboard layout, and full constructional details with instructions for testing the circuit at each stage. Each description ends with a list of the components required, all of which are readily obtainable. The appendix explains how to solder and how to build circuits on stripboard.

To obtain your copy, send your cheque
for £6.95 payable to PC Publishing to:

PC Publishing

4 Brook Street, Tonbridge, Kent TN9 2PJ *or*
✳ ring our credit card hotline, tel: 0732 770893 · fax: 0732 770268 ✳

How to set up a Home Recording Studio

David Mellor

126pp · ISBN 1 870775 30 9
£7.95 (inc P&P)

* Practical details on equipment, wiring and acoustics
* Glossary of terms, and lists of useful addresses
* Published in conjunction with Sound on Sound magazine

The book describes the setting up of a small studio with an outline of the musical and recording gear needed, but concentrating on the techniques of putting that equipment together into an efficient and productive home studio.

It contains invaluable and hard to come by advice on patchbay wiring and layout, information on cables and soldering and describes how to custom build a rack to suit your own particular requirements. There is a chapter on acoustics and layout, and appendices containing useful lists of equipment, distributors and manufacturers.

If you're thinking of setting up a studio, there's something in this book for you!

Contents
Equipment; Cables; Soldering techniques and wiring looms; Building a rack; Patchbay wiring; Patchbay layout; Studio acoustics and layout; Bits and pieces; Questions and answers; Advanced interconnection; Directory of manufacturers and distributors; Glossary of terms; Index.

'An invaluable accessory'
Musician magazine

To obtain your copy, send your cheque for £7.95 payable to PC Publishing to:

PC Publishing

4 Brook Street, Tonbridge, Kent TN9 2PJ *or*
✻ ring our credit card hotline, tel: 0732 770893 · fax: 0732 770268 ✻

If you have found this book useful, why not take a look at some
of our other titles. We publish a wide range of titles on electronics,
MIDI, home recording, audio and computers in music. Send for a
catalogue now.

Write to:

PC Publishing
4 Brook Street
Tonbridge
Kent TN9 2PJ

Tel 0732 770893
Fax 0732 770268